PENGUIN BOOKS

THE SIEGE WITHIN

Leslie Lopez is a native of Malaysia who has covered regional politics, business, and terrorism for a number of leading publications, including *The Wall Street Journal.* He has won awards for his reporting on the 1997 Asian economic crisis and the aftermath of Asia's deadly financial tsunami. He also led the paper's regional coverage on the growing threat from Islamic terrorists, breaking dozens of exclusive pieces that have helped bring greater understanding of the problems posed by religious militancy. Lopez remains active in the pursuit of exclusive stories and *The Siege Within* is yet another, this time in book-form. Lopez lives in Kuala Lumpur with his family.

THE SIEGE WITHIN

Leslie Lopez

PENGUIN BOOKS
An imprint of Penguin Random House

PENGUIN BOOKS

Penguin Books is an imprint of the Penguin Random House group of companies whose addresses can be found at global.penguinrandomhouse.com

Published by Penguin Random House SEA Pte Ltd
40 Penjuru Lane, #03-12, Block 2
Singapore 609216

Penguin Random House SEA

First published in Penguin Books by Penguin Random House SEA 2024

10 9 8 7 6 5 4 3 2 1

ISBN 9789815266313

Typeset in Garamond by MAP Systems, Bengaluru, India

www.penguin.sg

For Dad, Mum & Connie

Table of Contents

Prologue

Friday morning, 9 February 1996, was particularly sunny for equatorial Malaysia.

Scores of Malaysians were making their way out of the capital, Kuala Lumpur, ahead of a week-long holiday to celebrate festivals for two of the larger races in multiracial Malaysia—the Muslim Eid for the dominant Malay population and the Chinese Lunar New Year. In the extended break to follow shortly, both occasions would fall just days apart.

The mood was anything but festive in the Prime Minister's Department, a sprawling complex of traditional, ethnic-Malay styled structures on stilts. It was built on an exclusive, leafy hilltop precinct that overlooked the traffic snaking out of the city.

For the two most powerful Malaysian politicians there, it was a mix of tension, betrayal, and a deep, very deep, sense of uneasiness.

Clenching the day's edition of *The Asian Wall Street Journal* that led with a news report headlined 'Steel Fiasco May Rattle Malaysian Government', Deputy Prime Minister Anwar Ibrahim burst into his boss' office. Anwar quickly trailed the traditional Muslim greeting of as-salaam alaikum

(peace be upon you) with words that were at once a reminder, admonishment, and challenge: 'Sir, I told you we could not cover this up.' Then he handed over the newspaper.

Mahathir bin Mohamad, the Prime Minister himself, was seated behind his large, neat wooden desk. He dropped the Friday edition of *The New Straits Times*, the local English daily, and scanned the *AWSJ* carefully. Sullen-faced, Mahathir delivered his curt response: 'You leaked it to him,' as if that would settle the matter.

Two months later at the same complex, Anwar recounted the episode with Mahathir to a reporter, who immediately responded: 'You and I know that's not the case.'

'Try telling that to him,' Anwar replied, his voice tinged with resignation. The steel fiasco known as the Perwaja scandal had seriously undermined his relationship with Mahathir.

For the PM, it was a raw nerve. The showcase steel company was intended to be a pillar of his state-led industrialization drive that began shortly after he took the leadership in 1981.

But the project, like many others, ran into trouble because of widespread mismanagement and outright corruption. Perwaja became insolvent, burdened with more than USD 1 billion in accumulated losses and a debt load of more than USD 2.3 billion owed to local banking institutions, making it a systemic risk to the financial system if the government did not come to its aid.

The Perwaja debacle tracked many of the policy fiascos of the Mahathir era that, during its twenty-two years, had bounced from one financial scam to another, all disguised under the mantra of economic development. Similar to Perwaja, billions of dollars were poured into a big black hole of financially reckless ventures that showed little economic sense, if at all. Ventures into car manufacturing and ship

building had all failed spectacularly, as had Malaysia's highly misguided attempts to corner the international tin market and dabble in foreign-exchange trading.

In the months that followed the *AWSJ* exposé, which I had written, Mahathir would be persuaded by his closest business and political cronies that Anwar, his presumptive heir apparent, had become a clear and present danger.

A charismatic politician with populist leanings, Anwar quickly rose up the political ladder and, just as quickly, defined himself as the antithesis to Mahathir's brand of politics and business, often referred to as Malaysia Inc., a powerful grouping of businessmen from all sides of the ethnic divide, politicians, civil servants, and deep-state operatives who indirectly controlled large swathes of the Malaysian command-capitalist economy that Mahathir had created. This is where business and government worked together in development, the economy anchored on the so-called privatization programme. More than an outsider, he was widely viewed as a direct threat to the intricate web of patronage and racketeering that defined national politics, itself dictated by the narrow interests of the political elite, comprising parliamentarians, shadowy deep-state operatives, senior civil servants, regulators, businessmen, and media operators.

The growing intolerance towards Anwar boiled to the surface during the summer of 1997 when the regional economic crisis hit. Reckless spending on projects with little commercial sense was turning the Mahathir dream into a nightmare that was set to bring down the system. Anwar opposed the use of public funds to bail out Mahathir's cronies, whose projects were tottering under mountains of debt.

To keep intact the economic and political system Mahathir had built, Anwar had to be brought down at all costs.

In a carefully choreographed political assault unprecedented in Malaysian history, Mahathir served Anwar as an example of what would happen to those who opposed him, and trained the entire autocratic system that he had constructed against his one-time successor.

He first slapped on capital controls that sheltered the domestic financial markets, and particularly protected the local currency, the ringgit, from being traded in currency markets.

Shortly after that, Anwar was stripped of his deputy premier's position and sacked from the ruling United Malays National Organization (UMNO) political party of the time.

On 20 September 1998, balaclava-clad police special forces wielding M-16 assault rifles broke into his home in KL's Damansara Heights suburb and arrested him under the Internal Security Act, which allows for indefinite detention without trial. Bashed in jail by the serving police chief, Inspector-General Rahim Noor, a black-eyed Anwar was later dragged to court, found guilty of corruption and sodomy charges and sentenced to long jail terms.

Simply put, Mahathir weaponized the judicial and security arms of the government to terminate Anwar's political career.

Mahathir's assault on economic orthodoxy by pegging the currency was a crucial element in his campaign against Anwar. Without it, the ringgit, which was already under intense selling pressure, could have depreciated sharply, leading to the sort of economic strife that earlier, in May 1998, had brought down Indonesian strongman Suharto.

With Anwar out of the way, Mahathir was free to focus on providing lifeline after lifeline in public funds to bail out his cronies as well as his own family members, and present the picture that his economic and political legacy remained intact.

In fact, Malaysia's failure to learn from the hard lessons that markets had delivered to countries such as South Korea, as well as neighbouring Indonesia and Thailand, is exactly what led to the fiasco at the very storied 1Malaysia Development Berhad (1MDB). [*Berhad*, a Malay word, is used to denote a public limited company in Malaysia; its short form is Bhd.]

The 1MDB scandal has been framed in many ways.

For the new Malaysian government that came to power in 2018 and the key protagonists (there are many), the narrative was the triumph of good over evil. This version recounts how an unlikely cast of politicians, allegedly upright technocrats, businessmen, media operators, and activists came together to help expose what has been billed as one of the biggest swindles in financial history.

But much of this was laden with selective reporting, and compromised by memories coloured by hindsight, as well as efforts to shade the truth by assigning blame to some while ascribing credit to others.

The real story is much more complex. Altruism certainly did not motivate the protagonists in a scandalous epic that took place within a political system that had long been built on notoriously pervasive corruption.

1MDB, the brainchild of the now-disgraced and jailed former PM Najib Abdul Razak, was incorporated in April 2009 and first presented as an overseas strategic investment arm funded entirely with borrowed money. But the vehicle quickly morphed into a private political slush fund for Najib and his patronage-driven UMNO party.

The rapid build-up of highly leveraged borrowing only forced 1MDB and its key drivers to hatch more and more

shady financial schemes to finance its mounting debt that, at its peak, stood at close to USD 13 billion.

There was no running away for Najib and his financial henchman, Low Taek Jho, over their direct roles as chief perpetrators of the scandal. How these two men were directly responsible for the flow of 1MDB's billions of dollars of sleaze that barrelled through global financial pipelines has been documented in great detail by the US Department of Justice, and media reports that morphed into books.

It also forced the closure of an established bank in Switzerland and continues to shake the foundations of US banking powerhouse Goldman Sachs.

What has been missing in the good-over-evil narrative is what happened in Malaysia—'ground zero' of the 1MDB scandal. Money was raised within the Malaysian financial system and allowed to flow into global financial markets. It had to be authorized by regulators, given the green light by external accounting and law firms, and approved by compliance departments of financial institutions.

As Najib's political standing weakened due to the growing infighting in UMNO, his opponents moved to use the deepening financial debacle at 1MDB to push for his ouster, threatening to charge him with corruption. The anti-Najib protagonists were of the same breed that supported Mahathir's thwarting of Anwar. They were not interested in pushing for regime change, and instead, simply wanted change at the top, because many in government were complicit in the 1MDB scandal.

The plot failed when Najib sacked his sitting Attorney General, Abdul Gani Patail, and Deputy Premier Muhyiddin Yassin, who are widely considered to be the masterminds

behind the attempted coup. That left the political elite and vested-interest groups in the anti-Najib camp with little choice but to internationalize the 1MDB issue, leading to the US Department of Justice civil forfeiture suit, and the subsequent fall of the Najib-led government.

But the spectacular ejection of the Najib-led National Front coalition government, which ranked as the longest-serving most cohesive political alliance in the world that ruled Malaysia uninterrupted since independence in 1957, did not usher any political change. Hopes that the peaceful handover of power would tear away the cloak of secrecy that long allowed politicians and their financial henchmen and surrogates leech on schemes to extract national wealth did not happen.

What did was another cover up.

'Many people failed Malaysians over the 1MDB scandal. It wasn't just politicians like Najib and Jho Low. The civil servants, regulators, lawyers, bankers, and accountants are very much to blame for this scandal,' Anwar later noted in a conversation with a journalist, after he was released from his second jail term in 2018.

'The more accurately the story is told, why our checks and balances failed and who else was complicit, needs to come out because the country can't afford for this to happen again.'

My name is Leslie Lopez, and I am the reporter with whom Anwar shared details of that encounter in the PM's office more than two decades ago, as well as his thoughts upon his release from jail in 2018.

The following pages offer my reporting of the 1MDB affair and the siege Malaysia remains trapped in.

1

High Priestess of Finance
September 2009

Senior executives from the foreign exchange trading division of Malaysia's central bank, Bank Negara, were shaken by huge purchases of US dollars in the domestic currency market and quickly decided to halt the resultant selling pressure on the ringgit.

Surprisingly, their queries to forex dealers from the Kuala Lumpur–based operations of Deutsche Bank, who were behind the ringgit sell-down, went unanswered.

Malaysia-based bankers, both foreign and local, know that ignoring Bank Negara, or Negara as it is typically referred to, is done at one's peril. Armed with sweeping powers, the whiff of a possible audit by Negara can send shudders through the top management and directors of banking boards.

The reputation of Negara's forex trading division, however, was somewhat chequered, the damage self-inflicted.

Negara's image had been affected in the early 1990s by its own trading misadventures in international forex markets

that had racked up losses of more than USD 12 billion over bets on the British pound, which had trader George Soros on the opposite side of the trades. The Negara governor at that time, former Price Waterhouse managing partner Jaffar Hussein, would resign in April 1994 over the scandal, in a rare display of accountability in Malaysia. That, too, only after he insisted that Negara's face in forex markets, Nor Mohamed Yackop, resign first. Nor Mohamed was head of the forex trading division at the time.

The failed financial foray was a stain that could never be wiped away and several top Negara officials had openly vowed never again to set foot on the dealing floor of the central bank, with its forbidding, plain-concrete headquarters in the heart of KL's old administrative enclave.

Fast-forward to late 2009, Negara governor Zeti Akhtar Aziz was as shaken over the ringgit sell-down as her senior executives on the trading floor. But she would make an exception on that September afternoon.

As Negara's forex traders, on the 14th floor of the central bank, worked the phones to get some explanation from counterparts in Deutsche, Zeti made a surprise appearance and wasted no time ordering her chargers to stand down. Her voice quivering when trying to emphasize a point, Zeti told Negara's forex traders to facilitate the trades for the purchase of the US dollars, which amounted to MYR 3.8 billion, or roughly USD 1 billion, going by the prevailing exchange rate at the time. 'This is for the PM (prime minister),' one trader recalls her saying.

Dressed in her trademark deep blue baju kurung, a traditional Malay long smock and dress, Zeti said nothing else before returning to her penthouse office on the

17th floor, knowing full well that her instructions would be carried out to the letter.

The build-up of the US dollar positions on that day paved the way for state-owned 1MDB to move USD 1 billion out of the country for an investment in a British Virgin Islands (BVI) entity known as PetroSaudi International. It would sow the financial seeds for what would become history's most audacious and costly financial con that is still delivering aftershocks to this day.

At the time, the Negara forex traders knew something just wasn't right. They were warned by their counterparts in private banks in Singapore and Hong Kong that the trades were highly irregular, especially because the movement of funds this large, from a state-owned entity (1MDB) to a BVI concern (PetroSaudi), was being handled solely by a foreign bank, when Malaysia had many other established financial institutions that could have easily performed the trades.

There was more. One former Negara forex trader, who remembers the episode well, noted that 'her presence at the forex floor was already out of the ordinary. She could have just made the call to the department head or dispatched one of her deputy governors to approve the trades. This clearly was personal.'

But there was no way anyone could caution Zeti about her actions, especially not the forex boys in Negara's notorious currency trading division.

Since being appointed as the country's first woman central bank governor in May 2000, Zeti had meticulously curated a public persona of financial probity. The country's first female chief of the central bank presented herself as the monetary

guardian who would shun the more risky endeavours of her predecessors, such as the reckless dabbling in international forex markets. She claimed credit for consolidating the country's banks and before long was being held up as the saviour of Malaysia's near-broken banking sector. She also took credit for pushing Islamic banking in Malaysia and the region.

International recognition came quickly and Zeti basked in the limelight, assuming the cloak of some kind of high priestess of global central banking. She carefully cultivated Kuala Lumpur–based CEOs of foreign banks, who in turn spoke of her in glowing terms to financial journalists who would parachute into the country for the occasional Malaysia story. She was named Central Banker of 2005 by financial magazine *Euromoney*. In 2004, *The Banker*, a publication of the *Financial Times*, gave her the global award for central banker of the year. There were numerous other awards from regional financial magazines and local newspapers.

Was she destined for this greatness? Zeti's past provides contradictory messages.

Zeti Akhtar Aziz was born on 27 August 1947 in Johor Bahru, the capital of peninsular Malaysia's southernmost state, Johor. JB, as it is known, sits at the waterway known as the Straits of Johor, between the peninsula and Singapore. Zeti is the only child of parents from very proud and culturally rich backgrounds. Her father, Ungku Abdul Aziz bin Ungku Abdul Hamid, of Malay and Turkish descent, was a member of the Johor royal household. Ungku Aziz was vice chancellor of Malaysia's oldest institute of higher learning, University of Malaya, for two decades until 1988, as well as a prominent economist. Zeti's mother, Norazah Abdul Aziz,

also of Malay and Turkish descent, was a journalist of note and a fierce promoter of Malay culture.

Zeti grew up in a very privileged and progressive setting, studying in two of the top Catholic schools in Kuala Lumpur. On her mother's insistence, she learnt the Bharatnatyam, a traditional dance with roots in southern India, before graduating with a degree in economics at the University of Malaya. She then embarked on postgraduate education at the Wharton Business School of the University of Pennsylvania, where she completed her PhD in monetary and international economics in 1978. Following her PhD, she took up her first job as an analyst at the South East Asian Central Banks (SEACEN) Research and Training Centre.

She joined Negara in 1984 as the deputy manager in the economics department, a humdrum division that was a far cry from the real excitement of other departments such as financial surveillance, banking regulations, and currency operations.

It was around the same time that Negara, an independent central bank that commanded influence over the economy, was under attack by Mahathir, who had come to power three years earlier. Mahathir viewed the Negara governor of the time, Aziz Taha, as an overly conservative bureaucrat who did not share the PM's vision of a Malaysian economy forged by rapid industrialization, which the PM himself would engineer and oversee.

The tensions came to a head when Mahathir appointed his close friend and advisor Daim Zainuddin as Finance Minister in July 1984. Daim, who was heavily involved in a wide array of business ventures, wanted the central bank to allow banks to free up property lending and security transactions to

stimulate the real estate and share markets. Aziz, who frowned on speculative activities, favoured tighter supervision of the country's banks and advocated that lending should prioritize the infrastructure and manufacturing sectors.

Aziz lost the credit policy confrontation after Daim got Mahathir's backing. In April the following year, the new finance minister struck at the heart of Negara's authority when his ministry took direct control of the powerful Capital Issues Committee, a watchdog for share transactions and corporate mergers and takeovers that came directly under Aziz's supervision at the central bank. Two months later, Aziz would resign, giving both Mahathir and Daim unrestrained clout over the economy. As mentioned before, Jaffar Hussein, formerly of Price Waterhouse, would replace Aziz and break with central banking orthodoxy by venturing into the risky world of foreign exchange trading, a road that would culminate in his resignation in May 1994 following the huge losses incurred by Negara in international currency trading.

During this time, Zeti would move up the ranks. Between 1989 and 1994, she headed Negara's representative office in London, a plush position for a good performer but not a posting reserved for someone destined for the top office. She returned to Negara headquarters to fill the position of chief economist. Shortly after, Zeti became one of the bank's three assistant governors, one of the best tag teams Negara ever had after the removal of Aziz by Mahathir and Daim.

Ahmad Mohamed Don and his deputy, Fong Weng Pak, were easily the country's most respected bankers before they were appointed to the central bank by Anwar Ibrahim, who replaced Daim as Finance Minister in 1991. Along with Anwar's top officers in the Malaysian Finance Ministry,

Secretary-General Clifford Herbert and his deputy, Aris Othman, the four men moved carefully, under Anwar's political cover, to repair the economy.

By 1992, a year after Anwar took over the finance portfolio, Malaysia would snap away from posting budget deficits and swing to a surplus position in government finances. This trend was maintained until the regional currency crisis, which originated in Thailand, hit in July 1997.

Zeti was never part of Anwar's stable of renaissance economic managers, nor was she someone Mahathir considered a heavy hitter.

In the corridors of Negara, debate began to swirl that Nor Mohamed, the central bank's rogue currency chief who was forced to resign in 1994 in the aftermath of the forex losses, was being tapped by Mahathir to devise ways to shield the local currency against speculation. Malaysia's top two central bankers in Negara at the time, Governor Ahmad and Deputy Fong, themselves trained accountants, turned to their chief economist for advice on the all-important question: What would pegging the currency and introducing capital controls do to the economy?

According to Negara staffers, the governor and deputy did not have any strong position on the matter but accepted Zeti's arguments that the move would be seen as breaking away from economic orthodoxy, which would then hurt the country's international reputation.

On that advice, both men dug in their heels and in late August 1998, Ahmad Mohamed, as national monetary guardian under the country's Exchange Control Act, informed Mahathir that he would not sign the diktat authorizing capital controls. He tendered his resignation after Mahathir demanded it. In solidarity with his boss, Fong also resigned.

To fill the vacuum in the central bank, Mahathir appointed Zeti as acting governor. And the woman who was against capital controls as chief economist promptly signed the order as governor, exposing the duplicitous side to her character.

The consequences of Zeti's actions at the time were huge. It allowed Mahathir to execute a strategy to destroy Anwar, his designated heir, which set Malaysian politics on the troubled path that it remains mired in today.

Her presence at Negara's foreign exchange trading floor in late September 2009 also brought huge ramifications. Had Zeti allowed the forex dealers to do their job and halt the transfer of funds to PetroSaudi, the 1MDB debacle may have been avoided.

So, who was she doing it for? Her boss Najib?

It was personal, as one senior central banker suspected at the time. It was for Low.

2

Muscles the Gatekeeper 2001

For a man who was often the central strategist to the many political shadow ops during Mahathir's leadership, it was particularly chilling for Daim when he realized he was being targeted by the deep state in early 2001. So, he warned his senior business disciples that his phone calls were being wiretapped by the Special Branch (SB), the covert intelligence-gathering division of the national police, which was also tracking his moves. One senior disciple, who had just recovered from a heart-bypass at the time, recalls the instructions that came from their boss through a third party: 'No calls. No meetings and tie up all loose ends.'

First came Mahathir's snide public comments on how Daim had handled the corporate rescues of politically favoured businessmen and companies mauled by the Asian financial crisis that had hit the region three years earlier. Then came the open opposition to Daim's suggestions in weekly ministerial meetings.

The most enduring political relationship that had shaped modern Malaysia was on the rocks.

The diminutive Daim, taciturn, intensely private and fondly known as 'Muscles' to his acolytes because he punched well above his weight in both business and politics, could not put his finger on why Mahathir had soured on him. What Muscles did not realize was that, like Anwar, he had become a political threat.

Debate about Malaysia often revolves around the dynamics of Mahathir's relationship with his erstwhile heir apparent, Anwar, but the Daim dimension to the Malaysian story is rarely discussed. Understanding the relationship between Mahathir and Daim, who both hail from the northern Kedah state that borders southern Thailand, is crucial to the broader story and is very much central to the siege that Malaysia finds itself in today.

Mahathir took the reins of power in early 1981 with some very fixed ideas about what needed to be done for the country's ethnic Malay community. The same applied to the Malaysian economy—as far as the new PM was concerned, bureaucrats and technocrats had steered it into disrepair.

Affirmative action programmes designed to uplift the social status of the country's economically insecure Malays were moving at a snail's pace. Worse still, UMNO's finances were in a shambles and its continued reliance on a junior partner in the government coalition, the financially flush ethnic Chinese party known as the Malaysian Chinese Association (MCA), galled Mahathir to no end. Nothing short of an overhaul would do and Mahathir wasted no time. He knew what was needed but the doctor had to find someone ruthless enough to execute his ambitious plan. His businessman friend Daim fitted the bill.

For the nearly two decades of Mahathir's first stint as prime minister, the elfin and soft-spoken Daim had fitted neatly into a number of roles, ranging from informal trouble-shooter, to purse keeper for the ruling UMNO party, business guru and finance minister. But he is best known as the architect of the politically driven economic model that Mahathir had long desired for Malaysia. The model was very much like South Korea's, where the state would direct economic growth with the co-operation of private business. But it came with an all-important caveat: Businesses must exist at the sufferance of the state. Daim devised a neat way to achieve this. Under the country's ambitious privatization programme, Daim handpicked a group of ethnic Malay business professionals with backgrounds in law, accounting, stockbroking, and banking, and entrusted them to carry out quasi-national projects, the primary goal being the creation of a Malay entrepreneurial class. There was also a powerful political dimension to the economic imperative of creating this class. These professionals all had direct links to the ruling UMNO, and the business projects they ran would provide funds for the political organization's activities. Additionally, control of important levers of the economy, such as transportation, telecommunications, banking, infrastructure development, ports, and ship-building would be in the hands of powerful ethnic Malay interests.

Unlike Mahathir's beleaguered dive into heavy industries, Daim's privatization push proved to be a huge success. The cascade of privileges showered on entities central to UMNO's business empire, such as the publicly listed United Engineers Malaysia Bhd (UEM) and its parent entity, Renong Bhd, had a profound impact on the country's stock market. Criticisms over the increasing politicization of the Malaysian economy,

cronyism, and favouritism in the award of government contracts and other lucrative concessions were shrugged off. A lot of money was being made from the growing intertwining of business and government. The Malaysian stock exchange, at the time the region's largest bourse, boasted daily turnovers way higher than the amounts transacted on the New York Stock Exchange. Foreign portfolio investors just couldn't get enough of Malaysia.

Everything was coming along swimmingly. The great doctor had reshaped Malaysia. By the early 1990s, UMNO had its own money machine. It no longer had to go hat in hand to the junior MCA party. What's more, Mahathir and Daim had together produced a new entrepreneurial class—all ethnic Malay businessmen who were not only taking on their ethnic Chinese corporate rivals in Malaysia but also expanding their businesses to neighbouring countries such as Indonesia, Thailand, and the Philippines. The Malaysian economy rocked, UMNO was supreme and Mahathir called all the shots.

In March 1991, Mahathir reluctantly allowed Daim to resign from government but insisted he remain as UMNO's treasurer to oversee the continued expansion of the party's multibillion-dollar business enterprises. Anwar was appointed to the finance portfolio, in which he did a commendable job with the national finances, posting Malaysia's first budget surplus in more than two decades. But it was Daim who continued to get the credit for Malaysia's economic success, which was largely measured by the strong foreign investor interest in the country's supercharged stock market. His Midas touch was legendary. The slightest speculation that Daim was behind some deal was enough to trigger the violent

percolation of shares in the companies involved, which were listed on the Malaysian stock exchange.

It did not take long for hubris to set in.

So, when the central bank's entire capital base of over USD 5.5 billion was wiped out due to huge losses in international foreign exchange trades that went sour between 1992 and 1994, Mahathir and Daim, who had together sanctioned these highly unorthodox financial excursions by a central bank, refused to admit any fault or blame. Anwar bristled when the colossal losses, which were largely hidden from him, became public. Anwar vowed that there would be a full-scale investigation.

In a desperate attempt at damage control, Mahathir and Daim hastily hatched a corporate gambit to recapitalize Negara's balance sheet. They turned to a business crony representing UMNO, Tajudin Ramli, who had built up a profitable mobile telecommunications business. Mahathir and Daim directed Tajudin to acquire a controlling 32 per cent interest in national carrier Malaysia Airline System (MAS) that was held by the central bank. To help cover the central bank's capital losses, the airline's stock, listed on the Malaysian stock exchange, was acquired at a roughly 250 per cent premium over its prevailing trading price, valuing the whole deal at nearly USD 720 million. The controversial acquisition helped quell the growing public outcry over the forex losses at Negara and stopped Anwar's campaign for transparency over the debacle in its tracks. But this brazen corporate play, that appeared foolproof at the time, would resurface some years later to haunt the Mahathir-Daim machine.

When Mahathir and Anwar began to butt heads over economic strategy on how to deal with the fallout from

the regional financial crisis that began in mid-1997, Daim initially wavered over whose side he should take. In private conversations with close business associates and media executives, Daim shuddered at Mahathir's repeated railing of foreign currency speculators, which only depressed the value of the local ringgit. It also buffeted the stock exchange and pummelled the value of shares of the UMNO entities that had been used as collateral for bank borrowings. Renong alone stood as one of Malaysia's most debt-laden groups with borrowings of close to USD 3.5 billion. Daim sided with Anwar and often held private sessions with Mahathir, urging him not to rattle the markets.

But when the differences over economic policy broke out into a political fight between Mahathir and Anwar, Daim switched allegiances. Like Mahathir, he took the view that Anwar's austerity measures would end the rapid-growth policies that he and Mahathir favoured. Also, in peril were the many UMNO companies and the select few non-Malays, all of which had long fed on government-bestowed businesses and easy credit from a banking system that was largely controlled by the state.

A well-known Daim loyalist, A. Kadir Jasin, at the time editor-in-chief of the UMNO-controlled national daily, *The New Straits Times*, best described the Mahathir-Anwar conflict that divided Malaysia's political and corporate elite. Kadir told several of his senior media lieutenants that war had been declared between Mahathir and Anwar, and applied an interesting analogy to frame the looming confrontation, which was very much about control of Malaysia Inc. 'This is a fight between poachers and the gamekeeper. Daim is the gamekeeper and I will side with him,' Kadir told a select group of editors to ready themselves for the bruising national political battle that was to follow.

By late 1997, Mahathir brought Daim into the government and named him as chief of a new agency called the National Economic Action Council, which was tasked to map out a new game plan to salvage the Malaysian economy. The move firmly established the policy battle lines between Mahathir and Anwar. Six months later, Daim was appointed to the cabinet as special minister in charge of the economy.

The policy war with Anwar was over. Anwar's removal came quickly. In September that year, Anwar was sacked from office, jailed on charges of sexual misconduct and corruption.

Mahathir focused on repairing his badly mauled political standing, particularly among the country's ethnic Malays who were enraged by his treatment of Anwar. Shortly after, Daim was reappointed as finance minister and tasked with rebuilding UMNO's finances, which had been ravaged by the financial crisis, as well as weeding out businessmen and corporate groups considered to be aligned with Anwar.

Both men would stumble badly.

Mahathir's already-battered political prestige took a further drubbing when the politically dominant ethnic Malay community abandoned his ruling UMNO and rejected the party in droves in the November 1999 general election. The blame for erosion of support among the Malays was directed at Mahathir. His antagonists said he had increasingly dominated UMNO and surrounded himself with die-hard loyalists and business cronies who were disconnected from the struggles faced by the Malay community. Soon the question of how long Mahathir should lead the party became open debate.

Daim, who worked behind the scenes, was faring only a little better. He pushed ahead with bailouts of companies tied to UMNO and turned the screws on those associated with

the deposed Anwar, despite the backlash these actions had on the stock market. Businessmen such as Lim Thian Kiat of the sprawling Multi-Purpose Group were forced to cede control of their companies to entrepreneurs close to Daim. But nothing was more controversial than Daim's ambitious plan to push for the consolidation of Malaysia's fifty-eight financial institutions into six so-called anchor banks, all of which were either controlled by the state or his business allies. The plan made already-jittery investors more nervous. It did not appear that Malaysia had learnt any lessons from the financial crisis. To his detractors, Malaysia's paramount corporate gamekeeper was setting the stage for ultimate control. Not only was he seeking to make a large chunk of corporate Malaysia beholden to him, Daim also wanted to have a big say on the all-important role of determining who received access to the bank-lending that was the bedrock for any economy.

Many of the targeted business groups began to lobby other senior personalities in the Mahathir circle, particularly the prevailing central bank governor, Ali Abul Hassan Sulaiman, and Nor Mohamed, the once disgraced head of Negara's forex unit. Nor Mohamed's successful implementation of capital controls, a crucial element in Anwar's political assassination, brought him into Mahathir's inner circle, and he was quickly put in charge of several sensitive assignments that put him on a collision course with Daim.

Mahathir refused to accept that his political legitimacy had been seriously undermined. He was in denial about the irreparable damage to his legacy from his sacking of Anwar and the sham trials his former deputy faced on charges of sodomy and abuse of power. Instead, he warmed to whispers from both Ali and Nor Mohamed that Daim's corporate

machinations were a major stumbling block to repairing a battered economy and improving domestic and foreign investor sentiment, and Daim himself was becoming too powerful because of his fundraising role in a patronage-driven party. Daim represented a direct threat to the PM himself. The gamekeeper had to be neutralized.

Daim would soon learn that he had fallen out of favour with his long-time friend and chief patron, particularly after grumbling in UMNO grew louder over his oversteps. These included bailouts of his business associates, which involved outright awarding of government contracts that would raise funding to meet debt repayments, and directing banks to go easy pursuing loan defaults. UMNO warlords griped that Daim had turned a deaf ear to their own financial troubles, leaving a politically embattled Mahathir with no choice but to further distance himself from his long-time troubleshooter. The tipping point was the unravelling of a deal both Mahathir and Daim had devised years earlier, to get the government out of a financial pickle that Nor Mohamed had caused after the disastrous forays into global forex markets and the resultant losses of billions of dollars in public funds held by the central bank, Negara.

Of all the business cronies Mahathir and Daim nurtured, none feasted so well and fared more badly than Tajudin. The son of a rice farmer from the northern Kedah state that borders Thailand—where both his chief patrons hail from—Tajudin graduated with an economics degree from the University of Malaya in Kuala Lumpur. He worked in the government for a short while before he was recruited by Chase Manhattan (now JPMorgan Chase) to build its business in Malaysia in partnership with a local company called Amanah. He later moved to a merchant bank owned by the

state-controlled Urban Development Authority (UDA) that Mahathir had put under Daim's supervision. Shortly after that, Tajudin became a constant feature in Daim's corporate manoeuvres, often playing the role of partner and, later, that of Daim's business nominee.

Tajudin set up Technology Resources Industries Bhd (TRI) and in 1990 won a coveted four-year-monopoly to build a cellular telephone operation that became known as Celcom. The lucrative concession was awarded to Tajudin just a year before Daim resigned as finance minister. To build his cellular business, Tajudin began shedding other non-core assets such as a helicopter business and property concerns. This so-called telecommunications focus was easily sold by brokerage houses, both foreign and local, to their international clients, who at the time could not get enough of stocks in the emerging tiger economies. TRI stock climbed in the fifteen months between early 1992 and mid-1993 from less than one ringgit (roughly USD 0.40 at the prevailing exchange rates) to just under MYR 15.

But none of this bought him respect. Tajudin ranked low in the totem pole of Daim's established business protégés. He lacked the urbane tinge of superiority that an overseas education often distinguished Daim's first-tier of ethnic Malay professionals-cum-confidants—such as Razali Abdul Rahman, Hasan Abas, and Wan Azmi Wan Hamzah—from the others. He also lacked the swagger of Renong's cigar-chomping chieftain Halim Saad. He was always only seen as the quintessential ethnic Malay businessman who thrived on assistance from the state and measured no higher than a front man for his political masters.

To compensate for this, Tajudin turned to sporting expensive Italian suits, bought a yacht as well as a private

Gulfstream jet, and regularly granted media interviews to raise his profile, unlike Daim's other chargers who maintained a strict code of privacy.

When the government needed to be bailed out over the central bank's forex forays, Tajudin saw it as his opportunity to join the big league by stepping up to take over national carrier MAS and rescue Negara. Daim's other business disciples privately joked that Tajudin had just boarded a train that was heading for that proverbial wreck. They were right.

Tajudin suddenly became a poster child for all that was wrong with Malaysia when the financial crisis struck. The collapse in stock prices and the depreciation of the local ringgit hit businessmen like Tajudin, who were exposed to borrowing from local and foreign banks, and the punches rained with a ferocity that those in the privileged seats had never seen before. The cratering in the value of stocks in his listed entities that had been pledged as collateral for loans to local banks, combined with higher interest repayments for foreign borrowings because of the weakened currency, turned the businessman into one of the most indebted individuals in corporate Malaysia. That was not all. He also ran national airline MAS to the ground. When Tajudin took control of MAS, the airline boasted cash reserves of more than USD 240 million. By early 2000, MAS was riddled with mismanagement and saddled with more than USD 2 billion in accumulated losses.

In a nutshell, Tajudin became a systemic risk to the Malaysian financial system. If he were to be handed a financial lifeline, the bailout would bring the very real threat of triggering a domino effect that would scuttle the debt workouts of other UMNO-related assets, such as the Renong

conglomerate, and trip Malaysia's already-stretched financial markets into a freefall.

Left with limited options, Daim executed a partial rescue for Tajudin in late November 2000 by buying over the businessman's holdings in the troubled airline for USD 720 million, the same price Tajudin had acquired them for more than six years earlier. The crudeness of the bailout for Tajudin, at a time when scores of other businesses were struggling to stay afloat, further undermined Mahathir's waning political standing. The PM had signed off on the rescue plan, according to close associates of Daim, but when the political fallout became too much of a burden, Mahathir began to privately blame Daim for the country's economic woes. The likes of Ali and Nor Mohamed, who were hell-bent on getting rid of Daim, talked up narratives that the finance minister was sabotaging Mahathir's political standing with bailouts that only rescued his cronies, in moves that gave him greater control over the economy than the PM himself. The embattled Mahathir bought into the theory and readily gave the two civil servants—both of whom are Muslims of South Indian origin, or *Mamaks*, as Indian Muslims are often called in Malaysia—more latitude in economic and corporate decision-making.

To cut Muscles out of politics, the Mamaks turned the spotlight on his enormous wealth. Daim's business career, which stretches back to the late 1960s, was built on influence peddling, canny networking, and exploitation of the country's cosy and murky world of business and politics. Widely considered to be one of Malaysia's richest personalities, Daim's wealth has long been a cause of major debate and speculation. A former Renong senior executive, who used to enjoy unparalleled access to Daim, recalled Daim making a

trip to Bangkok in the early 1990s. Daim had used the private jet that belonged to Renong boss Halim Saad for a quick visit to meet his finance counterpart in the Thai cabinet. Daim gave the Renong charger a snapshot of a diamond-studded necklace he wanted collected from a top jeweller at a five-star hotel in downtown Bangkok. But the Daim trooper, who did not want to risk carrying such a valuable item in Bangkok, suggested that the jeweller personally deliver the item to Daim at the departure lounge for private jet passengers at the city's Don Muang airport. Daim was pleased to see his jeweller friend and praised his workmanship. When the question of payment arose, Daim suggested it would be as usual. He looked at the bill, flipped the single page over and scribbled: 'Bangkok Bank please pay.'

The government scrutiny of his personal wealth made Daim uneasy, particularly after Nor Mohamed and Ali ordered Negara to audit the former finance minister's little-known Swiss-based banking group, International Commercial Bank (ICB). ICB had opened its first branch in 1993 in the Czech Republic before expanding to other peculiar financial centres such as Prague, Budapest, and the African cities of Conakry and Accra.

Barely five months after the government's controversial takeover of the national airline MAS to bail out Tajudin, Mahathir announced that Daim would be taking an unprecedented two-month leave of absence. By early June, Daim was completely out of the picture, and a month later a Nor Mohamed–led operation formally initiated a takeover of the sprawling Renong Group by the government, a move that eventually gave ownership of the corporation to state-owned Khazanah Nasional Bhd.

This sweeping ownership change, at the heart of UMNO's one-time formidable political war chest and its mega-business interests, sowed the seeds of the twin curses that ail Malaysia to this day. The original aims of bringing greater transparency to the murky world of politics and business and restoring the country's tarred corporate governance report card were seen as little more than lip service for foreign investors. The takeover of Renong, and that of several other UMNO-related corporate entities that followed, has allowed the state to dominate the economy, thereby squeezing out private sector participation to drive growth. Over the last two decades, financial and economic manoeuvring have turned the country into the region's most underperforming economy. The more chilling consequence is the proliferation of schemes by Malaysian politicians to cover the funding gap for the country's entrenched multibillion-dollar political patronage networks, particularly within UMNO, leading to the outright looting of government coffers.

The Malaysian man on the street, and those who study this country in general terms, look at the series of financial scandals during Mahathir's twenty-two years in power as separate and unrelated events. In reality, the Mahathir era was nothing but a huge national swindle during which his government embarked on a series of scams, packaged as policy initiatives. These schemes, in areas such as banking, healthcare, state-owned manufacturing projects and real estate development, made profit-making for the political and business elite almost as assured as taxes. Mahathir's policies turned Malaysia into one of Southeast Asia's most corrupt nations. The country also became a lighthouse for scammers like Low.

3

The Hidden Hand

2004

Retirement was not going well for Mahathir, not well at all.

Barely three months after handing power to Abdullah Ahmad Badawi in end-October 2003, Mahathir realized he had made a huge mistake. Every decision by the new PM, on both the economic and political fronts, appeared to expose the failings of Mahathir's twenty-two-year rule.

To those who would listen, Mahathir griped that Badawi's group of unofficial advisors—led by his son, Kamaluddin Abdullah, and Khairy Jamaluddin, who would later become a member of the first family after marrying PM Abdullah's daughter—were behind a campaign to undermine his political legacy and target his economic agenda by going after long-time associates. 'There was hardly an occasion where he would fail to agonise about his decision to hand over to Abdullah,' said businessman Ananda Krishnan, a close associate of Mahathir and someone who would later play a major role in the 1MDB affair, in an interview.

And in the matters related directly to Mahathir, the taunting by the Abdullah administration manifested in many ways.

Abdullah's thumping election victory at the polls on 21 March 2004 was both the biggest electoral win in Malaysian history since independence from colonial Britain in 1957, and a major humiliation for Mahathir. Incumbent Abdullah's win reversed the losses suffered in the preceding years by the ruling National Front (Barisan Nasional in Malay) coalition, in which UMNO was the lead component. Those electoral setbacks had come under Mahathir's leadership and were, in large part, caused by Mahathir's sacking of Anwar, who was still a prisoner at the time of Abdullah's unprecedented level of voter endorsement.

Then came the assault on corruption. Eric Chia, a long-time Mahathir associate who had been handpicked by the latter in 1988 to revive the ailing fortunes of his showcase steel project, Perwaja, was hauled to court. My February 1996 exposé in *The Wall Street Journal* had singled out Chia for huge management abuses that had led to the collapse of the steelmaker. Nothing had happened to him under Mahathir's watch, but the Abdullah government discovered new evidence and charged Chia.

Barely days after Chia was charged, Abdullah's government took aim at prestige projects awarded by Mahathir to Syed Mokhtar Albukhary, a businessman who, in the late 1990s, had emerged as Mahathir's corporate son of choice. Abdullah's government indefinitely shelved the construction of a USD 4 billion electrified double-track railway line that would have stretched the length of peninsular Malaysia. The project, easily the largest ever privatization venture in

Malaysia's history, was awarded to Syed Mokhtar just days before Mahathir resigned.

The assault on Syed Mokhtar's businesses continued with the cancellation of another privatization award—a controlling stake in a dam project valued at just under USD 2 billion in the east Malaysian state of Sarawak.

Mahathir bristled, but there was little he could do.

Two oceans away, Low, an undergraduate at the Wharton Business School in the University of Pennsylvania (where former Negara governor Zeti had completed her PhD in 1978), was paving the way to make a return to his home country. The country's bumpy leadership succession provided an opening.

Low reasoned that Abdullah's courting of Saudi Arabia and the United Arab Emirates (UAE), under a new diplomatic initiative to lure investments for the local economy, was something he could exploit. Low knew the players in both Middle Eastern countries well, or at least he knew the children of the wealthy and powerful in both Saudi Arabia and the UAE, particularly Abu Dhabi.

Low had *wasta*, loads of it. In the Arab world, *wasta*, which means connections or clout, was the single most important ingredient to get ahead. Malaysia was no different. The mixing of business and politics was a central theme in the country's development. Low, who was a native of Malaysia's northern resort island of Penang, figured that he could bring these two worlds together and profit from it.

Low was twenty-three in mid-2004 when he decided to take a break during his final year in Wharton, return to Malaysia, and set up Wynton Capital, his boutique investment company. With real estate assets from a

Penang-based businessman close to the family, Low raised the seed capital for his new venture and brought together a team of professionals to scour for takeover targets in the shifting sands of corporate Malaysia. Low drafted Nikolai Dobberstein, the former managing partner of McKinsey & Company in Malaysia, and fund manager Omar Merican, whose father was one of Malaysia's most respected civil-servant-turned-merchant bankers.

The political muscle for Wynton Capital came from Nizam Razak, a former CEO of a local stockbroking company and younger brother to the deputy PM of that time, Najib, whose father had been Malaysia's second prime minister.

While Team Low did not boast of any big-league hitters in Malaysia's corporate deal-making scene, they quickly spotted an opening in the unfolding Abdullah-Mahathir spat, which was fast shaping into a bare-knuckle political brawl.

Sometime in mid-2004, a pivotal block of shares in publicly listed DRB-Hicom (a merger of a state entity and private holding, which we will come to later) came up for grabs. It caught the eye of Low and his team.

Ordinarily, DRB-Hicom would have attracted numerous suitors, both local and foreign. It was poorly managed and riddled with leakages. But it was also asset-rich and enjoyed a political pedigree unmatched in corporate Malaysia—both elements that, brought together, made it an excellent takeover target with potential for a very viable turnaround. But this was no ordinary concern. DRB-Hicom was Mahathir. He created Heavy Industries Corp. of Malaysia, or Hicom, in 1980, when he was deputy PM.

A year later, after taking over the country's top job, Mahathir made it the centrepiece of his push to turn

commodity-dependent Malaysia into a nation of heavy industrialization. To realize this, he embarked on joint ventures between his government and Japanese companies to create a national car maker, establish both a steel-making plant network and cement production facilities, and put together defence-related initiatives, from the assembly of military vehicles to brokering large arms contracts.

Hicom was also Mahathir's personal piggy bank, and it served as his private slush fund during his early years in power. The groundbreaking ceremonies of the cement facility, steel plants, and the car manufacturer, Proton, were all lavish political affairs and broadcast nationally to shore up Mahathir's political prestige. Ordinary folks were bussed in from rural hamlets and enticed with free meals and pocket-money for the inconvenience. All these events were paid for by the government, while parcels of the construction work went to political supporters who secured inflated contracts that were poorly executed, and often resulted in cost overruns.

Barely seven years later, the Mahathir administration would have to admit that the push into heavy industries had been a colossal failure. Every single venture had failed. Hundreds of millions of ringgit in public funds had been squandered due to bad management and outright embezzlement.

Undeterred, Mahathir restructured Hicom. He changed the management at its key divisions and ploughed more taxpayer money into the ventures. It appeared at the time that Malaysia could afford another stab at Mahathir's industrialization push. After all, the country was entering a period of unprecedented economic growth that had begun in the late 1980s and early '90s on the back of rising commodity prices and a fast-expanding manufacturing sector, particularly

in the electrical and semi-conductor fields. Malaysia was emerging as one of the next tiger economies to join the ranks of South Korea.

But the successes of South Korea's industrialization push eluded Malaysia. Hicom's cement factory was suffering losses due to production problems. There were more horrors in Perwaja. The steel company had become technically insolvent. Anwar, who was at the time the country's finance minister, decided that the haemorrhaging of national coffers caused by the Hicom projects had to stop. Anwar appointed accounting firm Price Waterhouse to conduct a due diligence audit on the steelmaker, which was exposed as nothing but a national dud. The Perwaja that was supposed to produce high-end steel billets for the construction sector and steel sheets for car-manufacturing could only produce nails, screws, and hammers at best.

With advance knowledge of the Price Waterhouse audit, Mahathir knew it was only a matter of time before the same prying eyes (among the loyalists of the Anwar-led finance ministry) would reach carmaker Proton. Mahathir was particularly passionate about Proton and he had made it clear from the start that the carmaker was his to manage, and to sign off on for all major decisions. But as the Perwaja debacle rocked his administration, speculation began to swirl that similar shenanigans were taking place in the form of bloated vendor deals where politically connected companies were profiting from the sale of parts and components to the carmaker. Hundreds of millions of ringgit in government grants for automotive research at Proton would be outsourced to acolytes of Mahathir, particularly to Frazer-Nash, an engineering concern in the UK that was at the time owned by

Indian businessman Kamal Siddiqi, who enjoyed very warm ties with the Malaysian PM.

In October 1995, five months before the Perwaja scandal was exposed by *The Asian Wall Street Journal*, Mahathir engineered the government's sale of a controlling stake in Hicom, which came along with interests in concerns such as carmaker Proton, a national car-distribution network known as EON, a cement maker and finance arm. Continuing his programme of privatizing state assets, Mahathir tapped businessman Yahya Ahmad, who was already running an auto assembly operation, DRB, to take control of the government-owned entity. The new group was called DRB-Hicom, representing the merger of Yahya's Diversified Resources Bhd and the state entity.

By all accounts, Yahya, who studied automotive engineering in the UK, did a commendable job whipping Proton into shape and quickly became Mahathir's most important troubleshooter. He was often assigned to salvage troubled projects that the PM had regularly approved for his cronies with little scrutiny or study. Apart from his growing closeness to Mahathir, Yahya was also a close friend and schoolmate of Anwar, the combination of which alarmed many sections of UMNO and the business community. Speculation began to swirl that Mahathir was setting the roadmap for his succession.

But Malaysia Inc. was not ready for a handover. Of particular concern to Mahathir's political and business acolytes was Anwar's determined war against corruption. Much of corporate Malaysia's wealth during the Mahathir years was grounded on the mixing of politics and business, which created extraordinary riches for an elite group. They faced no real competition in a system that was rigged.

Anwar was aware of the budding opposition to his rise, but there was little his detractors could do as long as he was on Mahathir's good side. Then there was Yahya, who was increasingly becoming someone Mahathir favoured over older cronies such as Vincent Tan and Malaysian tycoon T. Ananda Krishnan.

Yahya was among a small group of ethnic Malay businessmen who regularly met at Anwar's official residence after dinner to discuss national economic issues and politics. On 2 March 1997, during one of these regular sessions, Yahya received an urgent call that said his ailing mother's condition had worsened. Breaking the news to Anwar, Yahya told him that he had to leave immediately for the capital of the north-eastern state of Terengganu on his private helicopter. He also apologized to Anwar, who was supposed to use that same helicopter in the coming days for a quick political event just outside Kuala Lumpur; Anwar would have to arrange some other form of transport.

Well before the morning twilight prayers of *suboh*, the first of the five supplications Muslims observe each day, news broke that Yahya's helicopter had crashed in the rugged terrain of the main Titiwangsa mountain range that divided much of peninsular Malaysia's east and west. The crash killed Yahya, his wife Rohana Othman, and two others, the pilot and Yahya's bodyguard. The charred bodies of Yahya and Rohana were discovered locked in embrace. Was there foul play? Yahya's closest lieutenants never dismissed that possibility. But the question remains: Was it planned for Yahya or Anwar?

In any case, Yahya's closest aides gave the news to Anwar in the early hours of that tragic March morning. Anwar decided he would inform Mahathir personally. His boss took

the news badly. Mahathir wept. But there was little time to grieve, especially when a key vestige of his troubled heavy industry push was now lost forever.

Shortly after Anwar informed Mahathir of Yahya's death, a group of operatives from the Special Branch broke into Yahya's private office in downtown Kuala Lumpur and ransacked it, raiding his safe. Yahya's corporate lieutenants, who were scrambling to deal with the immediate fallout from their boss' death, wondered what the authorities could be looking for. That the Special Branch detail was after details of Yahya's controlling stake in DRB-Hicom would only become apparent later.

Yahya had been careful. He had made sure that, in the event of his passing, his controlling interest would be transferred to a family trust, and management of the group would be handed over to his long-time business partner, Saleh Sulong.

But the fortunes of DRB-Hicom slid sharply following Yahya's passing and the regional economic crisis that hit in mid-1997. Mahathir refused to acknowledge that his costly economic experiment in heavy industries was a policy fiasco.

Raising funds to cut the group's growing debt load, Mahathir directed the country's cash-rich national oil corporation, Petronas, or Petroliam Nasional Bhd, to take control of Proton, wresting it from DRB-Hicom in a bid to keep the national car project viable. In the meantime, DRB-Hicom kept snaring potentially lucrative business concessions from the government to stay afloat. None worked and the group's debts kept ballooning.

By the time Mahathir surrendered his leadership in late 2003, DRB-Hicom had become an unresolved component of his legacy.

In March 2004, Yahya's family trust, which had held the controlling stake in DRB-Hicom following his death, defaulted on loans it owed to several Malaysian banks. But financial institutions could not simply toss the block out in the open market, or dispose of it to the highest bidder. Apart from the powerful Mahathir connection, the Malaysian government also controlled a roughly 30 per cent component in the group. Corporate suitors had to secure the government's blessing before mounting a bid.

Mahathir turned to his favourite crony to make a bid for the company. This was none other than Syed Mokhtar, who, as stated earlier, was facing a series of setbacks with the Badawi government's cancellations of projects awarded by the previous (Mahathir) administration. But there was unease in the new Abdullah administration about Syed Mokhtar's acquisitive streak, which had begun in the twilight of Mahathir's time in office. Syed Mokhtar's expansion into areas such as ports, power generation, hotels, manufacturing, and sugar refining was based entirely on borrowings from the local financial system. In turn, this gave rise to concerns that his debt-heavy group could pose another systemic threat to the country's financial structure in the event of a serious economic downturn.

Enter Team Low. The Wharton undergrad with loads of *wasta* never did show his hand in the takeover bid for DRB-Hicom and his role has not been disclosed until now. But in the course of the corporate battle for the conglomerate, he displayed his clout by getting potential investors from Abu Dhabi and Saudi Arabia to visit the company, so as to show that the Wynton Capital bid had solid international backing. He was also slowly building on other connections with people

associated to the Wharton alumni, particularly Malaysia's central bank governor at the time, Zeti Akhtar Aziz, and her husband, Tawfiq Ayman.

The competing bid caught the attention of Abdullah's core team of advisors. There was a political angle. They were keen to woo Low's front-man, Nizam, in a bid to forge closer political ties with Nizam's brother, Najib, who at this point was deputy PM and a powerful warlord in UMNO.

But Nizam did not pack the kind of punch to take on the likes of Syed Mokhtar. Nizam's record in corporate Malaysia was also somewhat tarred. A stockbroking firm he headed had taken a spectacular loss over trades with a very suspect businessman during the 1997–98 regional crisis. To beef-up the challenge, Team Low was encouraged by Abdullah's advisors to bring in businessman Nasimuddin Amin, who at the time was one of Malaysia's most successful auto distributors, as their corporate face.

A crucial turning point would come on 2 September 2004, when Malaysia's Federal Court unexpectedly reversed the conviction of Mahathir's former deputy-turned-political-nemesis, Anwar. Mahathir believed that Abdullah had a hand in the verdict and, to the former PM, war had been declared.

DRB-Hicom now became a battle Mahathir could not afford to lose. Too much was at stake and Mahathir feared that a change of ownership to a less than friendly individual could lead to disclosures of troubles in the group, further sullying his legacy.

It is 3 December 2004. In the hours before the obligatory mid-day Friday prayers for Muslims, Abdullah's chief press

secretary, Kamal Khalid, is to alert his media buddies in the local and foreign press that the PM has made a decision on DRB-Hicom. The press release has been prepared. The intensely contested stake in DRB-Hicom is to go to the Nasimuddin team that is, for all practical purposes, led by Low.

But things are to change very quickly. Abdullah would walk into his office after prayers and bluntly tell Kamal that he has changed his mind. 'It [the DRB-Hicom Group] is going to Syed Mokhtar. I have decided,' is all he says to his stunned press secretary.

Abdullah did not tell his aides why he changed his mind, but they suspect Mahathir has made a direct call to their boss to read him the riot act about the very apparent undermining of his legacy. It is more than likely that Mahathir has very much ordered Abdullah to approve Syed Mokhtar's bid.

The news that afternoon stuns the Nasimuddin team. Low, who has been working behind the scenes, does not take the setback well. He quickly turns to his close friend, Zeti. By this time, Low is a regular guest at Zeti's home in the tree-lined and prestigious Taman Duta suburb in Kuala Lumpur, the same precinct where Abdullah's deputy, Najib, has his home.

Low tells Zeti she needs to intervene as the central bank governor, on the grounds that Mahathir's meddling in government affairs will undermine foreign investor sentiment. Zeti wants to curry favour with the Abdullah administration. The construction of a new central bank office block that the governor has chosen to personally oversee is plagued by irregularities in the contract award, and it has begun to attract the attention of Abdullah's officers. In a bid to head

off the unwanted scrutiny, Zeti decides to take one for the team and moves on her own to throw a wrench into the DRB-Hicom deal.

In an unprecedented move, Bank Negara orders banks and law firms representing Syed Mokhtar in the acquisition of the block of shares held by Yahya's family trust to disclose how he intends to fund the purchase. There is good reason to be concerned. Syed Mokhtar's fast-expanding corporate kingdom at the time boasts assets that have controlling stakes in a port operation, power plants, real estate, and manufacturing, all built on the back of little-known private companies, many of which do not disclose any direct links to him in public records. As Mahathir's most favoured corporate son, banks and Malaysia's regulatory agencies have viewed his deal-making moves with soft focus. But with Mahathir no longer in office, Low and his team are hoping that Bank Negara's disclosure demands for the DRB-Hicom transaction will trip Syed Mohktar's bid.

It will take a whole month before Bank Negara allows Syed Mokhtar to proceed with the deal. The approval is not based on the disclosures about funding by Syed Mokhtar's banks and law firms. It's come simply on the back of his unrivalled political clout.

It is an important lesson for Low as he plots his homecoming. In a country where political connections count, Low's wasta has proved to be wanting. Ties to the likes of Zeti are not going to be enough.

4

Homecoming 2006

Low bounced back quickly from the setback in the bid for DRB-Hicom. He returned to Philadelphia to complete his degree at Wharton, while his partners in Kuala Lumpur scouted for fresh deals. By the first quarter of 2006, he had returned to Malaysia, where he would often shuttle between KL and Georgetown, his hometown in the northern Malaysia island of Penang. He also made regular trips to Abu Dhabi to woo state funds there to consider investing in Malaysia.

The first order of business was beefing up his wasta. Low moved quickly to enlist new shareholders for his private corporate vehicle, Wynton Capital, and tapped on the royal households of both Kuwait and Abu Dhabi, the latter being the wealthiest of the seven sheikhdoms that make up the UAE.

In Wynton Capital:

- Sheikh Nasser Sabah Al-Ahmad Al-Sabah, a shareholder and director of Kuwait Projects Company, or KIPCO, the gulf state's powerful investment arm with assets of over USD 33 billion, took a 20 per cent interest.
- Sheik Khaled Mohamed Zayed Al-Nahyan, a member of UAE's ruling royal family in the gulf, and Yousef Mana Saeed Al Otaiba, who was another senior member of the UAE's political elite, collectively took a 20 per cent interest.
- Malaysian shareholders were led by Najib's younger brother, Nizam, with a 25 per cent interest.
- Nooni Mahmood, the sister-in-law to Badawi, the prime minister, held a 10 per cent interest.
- Tawfiq Ayman, the husband to the powerful central bank governor Zeti, settled with 5 per cent.
- The remaining 20 per cent was held by Wynton Private Equity Group (Global) BVI Ltd, a shell company controlled by Low in the tax haven of the British Virgin Islands.

To better reflect the shareholding make up, the company was renamed ADKMIC, which stood for Abu Dhabi-Kuwait-Malaysia Investment Corp. Low also wanted to feature some cross-border clout. ADKMIC created a separate corporate vehicle, incorporated in Malaysia, called Swan Symphony, and Low brought in Autron Corp Ltd as a 49 per cent partner. At the time, Autron was an entity incorporated in Australia that enjoyed a dual listing on the Australian Stock Exchange and the Singapore bourse.

Autron, which was involved in the electronics sector with plants in Singapore, Malaysia, and China, was proposing to move into real estate. The driving force of the company was Eric Lim. The Autron board of directors featured several prominent Singaporeans, including Professor Hang Chang Chieh of the National University of Singapore and Ho Sing, who was appointed advisor to the board. Ho Sing is the younger brother of Ho Ching, wife of Singapore Prime Minister Lee Hsien Loong and easily Singapore's most influential corporate personality.

The other ace up Low's sleeve was his close friendship with Khaldoon Khalifa Al Mubarak, one of the most trusted advisors of the Al Nahyan family that ruled Abu Dhabi. He is also the chief executive officer of the Mubadala Investment Company, a state-owned investment holding company with assets exceeding USD 230 billion.

Low then moved to strengthen his deal-making team. He found that his first set of financial lieutenants was too strait-laced for his liking. Seduced by the go-go deal-making that defined corporate America, which was part of his business case studies at Wharton, Low reckoned that he needed a team of young whippersnapper financial whiz kids.

He was looking for people who shared his thrill of structuring corporate deals financed by debt. His plan was to set up companies with opaque ownership structures underpinned by a labyrinth of private shell companies in tax havens, and to then flip those companies like tortillas.

It wasn't about skirting very close to the edge of what was legal, but vaulting over the hurdles in his way with complex, toxic, and structured deals. With cunning and a practised sleight of hand, the entities would appear legitimate on the surface. Why build a business, when you can take over

existing companies with debt and flip them for a profit? That was Low's motto.

This was the beginning of the aforementioned Team Low, and the mastermind didn't have to go far to put it together. Schoolmates from Penang and friendships he had made during his freshman years in the United Kingdom, and later at Wharton, provided a ready pool of talent.

Before long, Low's close ties to the wealthy Arab set became known to political fixers and corporate dealmakers in Malaysia.

One of the first serious connections Low established was with a group called Cahya Mata Sarawak (CMS). An industrial powerhouse in Sarawak, a resource-rich Malaysian state in the rugged regions of northwest Borneo, CMS was owned directly by the family of Taib Mahmud, the state's chief minister at the time (the family still owns CMS).

Taib, a flamboyant silver-maned politician, boasted a penchant for all things expensive, such as vintage Rolls Royce limousines. At his sprawling mansion just outside the state capital of Kuching, a grand piano once owned by flamboyant American pianist Liberace would come to grace a huge living area dripping with gaudy vases on cabinets, replete with gold detailing. At the same time, the chief minister possessed tasteful and exquisite Persian silk carpets.

But for all of Taib's political heft in Malaysia's political landscape, CMS was facing serious problems with one of its prized investments, RHB Group, which was then Malaysia's fourth largest bank.

Here, again, Malaysia's high priestess of finance would leave behind a trail of meddling. For reasons still unclear, Zeti had taken an intense distaste to the CMS group, which controlled a

commanding 32 per cent interest in RHB. Zeti directed her ire at Taib's son, Sulaiman Abdul Rahman Taib, who ran RHB.

Zeti went out of her way to frustrate Sulaiman, often crossing the lines of an impartial regulator with arbitrary edicts. Nominees for a new chief executive officer and board appointments submitted by Sulaiman were summarily rejected by Zeti, who instead favoured candidates promoted by RHB's second largest shareholder, Malaysia's federally owned national pension vehicle, Employees Provident Fund (EPF). A move to rebrand RHB was turned down without reason.

Significantly, when CMS applied to settle a government loan ahead of schedule, Zeti's Negara demanded a 60 per cent premium on the outstanding loan of MYR 1 billion (roughly USD 250 million at the time). The demand by Malaysia's central bank was unprecedented in the recent history of Malaysia's banking sector. The message was clear: Zeti wanted CMS out of RHB.

But the Taib family that had long ruled Sarawak as a personal fiefdom and was so accustomed to getting its way could not accept being shown the door.

Low's close ties with Zeti and her husband, Tawfiq, got the attention of the top management at CMS, who reached out to the little-known corporate executive with strong Middle Eastern connections. Low recalls being approached by Ian Sadler, who at the time was the chief marketing officer at CMS, to help work out a structure that would allow CMS to retain control of RHB.

At the time, Low had already begun discussing business deals with the top management of the Kuwait Finance House (KFH) outpost in Kuala Lumpur, which was eager to buy its way into a financial institution in Malaysia.

Low, who was just turning twenty-five at the time, saw RHB as an ideal vehicle to leverage his strong Middle East connections and bring in the foreign direct investment that Badawi's government was eager to attract. In Low's mind, RHB would be a bank with sizable Middle Eastern equity, and it would help attract investment not just for Malaysia but for neighbouring countries such as Thailand and Indonesia as well.

Low's multi-stage corporate exercise for RHB was both ambitious and audacious, and that was exactly why both Sarawak's CMS and KFH quickly saw how they could profit. 'Low pitched [RHB] as a huge onion and with each peel there was money to be made,' recalls a banker who was involved as an advisor to the deal.

The first part was easy enough. To ease the tension between Zeti and CMS, Low suggested that the Sarawak concern sell its commanding interest in RHB to KFH. He argued that the deal would be positive public relations coup for the Badawi government, which at the time was facing serious slippages to its popularity. Badawi's waning political capital was bleeding because he was failing to deliver on reform pledges.

Phase two of the corporate exercise was more tricky. Low's plan called for Abdullah's government to direct EPF to sell its roughly 31 per cent interest in RHB to a new Arab investor. Low had made overtures to the Abu Dhabi Commercial Bank, the third largest lender in the UAE, to consider buying EPF's interest. The deal would result in the Middle Eastern investors controlling more than 60 per cent of the financial institution. Low's plan also called for the immediate remodelling of the shareholding structure to comply with Negara's state policy of capping the equity investor in financial institutions at

20 per cent, a reorganization that would pave the way for Taib's family to come back as a shareholder.

'We were babysitting so many different groups,' Low recalls. 'There was Abdullah (Badawi), who Nooni was handling, while I worked on Zeti and the Arabs.' Nooni was Badawi's sister-in-law, whom Low had already drafted as a shareholder in his financial vehicle ADKMIC.

There was huge money to be made. Licences for financial institutions were not easy to come by and, because of the shareholding limits on foreign investors, a bank like RHB—which boasted an extensive network of branches in Malaysia as well as an operation in Singapore—would fetch a huge premium. But the broad picture of Low's plan leaked, and national pension fund EPF lobbied Badawi with a counter-proposal that would see it lead the restructuring plan. Low's scheming faced another problem: Zeti's exuberance in supporting his plan. Abdullah's core team of advisors, led by his son-in-law, Khairy, had taken a dim view of the central bank governor. They did not take kindly to her alleged complicity in a building project initiated by Negara that, potential bidders had privately complained, was riddled with possible favouritism towards a particular contractor short on experience, but purportedly long on cosy ties to Zeti's husband. All of this raised red flags in the PM's office, resulting in Badawi leaning in favour of the EPF-led deal.

With the benefit of hindsight, it was the right move. EPF went ahead to buy the Utama Banking Group (UBG) stake in RHB for MYR 2.25 billion, raising the pension fund's stake in the bank to over 57 per cent in March 2008. The following May, the fund sold a 25 per cent interest in RHB to Abu Dhabi Commercial Bank for MYR 3.88 billion.

5

Finding the Right Bank 2007

The consecutive setbacks—DRB-Hicom and EPF-RHB deals—did not deter Low. Rather than trying to package deals for others, Low decided he would get his hands muddied.

Finding the right bank was going to be crucial. It had to be a financial institution hungry enough to participate in schemes that most high-street outfits would not touch with a bargepole.

State-controlled Malayan Banking (Maybank) and Commerce International Merchant Bankers (CIMB), the country's top two financial groups, were the first to be scratched from the checklist Low and his advisors had drawn up. Low simply did not have the track record or credit standing to qualify as one of their corporate clients.

The Hong Leong Banking (HLB) group and Public Bank, two conservative financial institutions owned by ethnic Chinese tycoons, were next to be dropped from the list. Hong Leong and Public Bank were unlikely to fall for the financial

schemes Low was planning to structure because each would risk coming under the glare of the central bank, as well as Malaysia's ethnic Malay-led government, which had long wanted to limit the role of Chinese bankers in the economy.

The elimination process left two institutions on the checklist: AmBank Bhd, which was controlled by veteran banker Azman Hashim, and RHB Bank Bhd, majority-owned by the country's pension fund, EPF.

Team Low settled for AmBank. It was an interesting choice for several reasons. Similar to Low's newly minted ADKMIC, AmBank's origin went back to a collaboration between Middle Eastern and Malaysian interests in the mid-1970s. At the time, intrepid financier and entrepreneur Hussain Najadi was leading a high-powered delegation comprising politicians and businessmen from Kuwait, Bahrain, Qatar, Saudi Arabia, and UAE to the southeast Asian region. Singapore was the first stop, followed by Indonesia, Philippines and, finally, Malaysia. Here, the visitors met with the country's second prime minister, Abdul Razak Hussein. Four decades later, Razak's son, Najib, would also make it to the country's top job and come to work closely with Low.

The Najadi-led delegation was warmly received by Razak and his no-nonsense central bank governor, Ismail Ali, who was known to sack any officer on the merest hint of corrupt behaviour. Razak noted that his government was keen to build both political and economic ties with the Gulf states. Najadi seized on the opening and argued that the best way was to start a licensed bank, which would launch as a merchant bank and later transform into a commercial bank. He argued that surplus money held by Gulf banks could fund infrastructure development and spur economic activity.

Negara governor Ismail convinced Razak it was a good idea and, within months, Arab Malaysian Development Bank (AMDB) was incorporated. The entity was owned by the Malaysian government, which controlled 55 per cent. The remaining 45 per cent was held by a Kuwaiti Investment firm that Najadi had set up earlier, Arab Investments for Asia Kuwait Ltd (AIAK).

With Najadi helming Arab Malaysian, the financial institution quickly stamped its mark on the local banking scene. Backed by solid government connections both in Malaysia and Kuwait, Arab Malaysian quickly secured mandates to arrange syndicated loans for national oil company Petronas, national air carrier Malaysia Airlines (MAS), and the Malaysian government itself.

But the stifling regulatory parameters on the banking sector began to discourage Najadi. In 1982, he sold all his shares in Arab Malaysian to its current owner, Azman Hashim, who at the time was the executive director of Maybank. Just after exiting Arab Malaysian, Najadi's fortune turned quickly. His return to his homeland of Bahrain to operate a separate financial institution ended in misery. He was jailed for seven years after committing the unthinkable in the autocratic state: Najadi crossed the royal family when he insisted that one of its senior members repay a loan from his bank that had not been serviced for nearly a decade.

Najadi eventually returned to Malaysia in 2002, maintained a strict distance from Arab Malaysian and started a financial consultancy business that was modestly profitable.

But Najadi's life would end tragically eleven years later, on 29 July 2013, when he was assassinated by a drugged-up hired gunman 'with very blurred vision'. The shooting was

at a parking lot next to the Arab Malaysian headquarters in downtown Kuala Lumpur. More on this episode will be revealed in later pages.

While Najadi was wallowing in a Bahraini prison, banker Azman was embarking on an expansion of the Arab Malaysian franchise, a growth strategy that would last more than a decade. To realize his vision, Azman acquired a finance company, a securities firm, a leasing concern, and eventually a commercial bank, all grouped under the publicly listed Arab-Malaysian Merchant Bank Holdings (AMMB). A separate listed entity called Amcorp Berhad, which controlled Azman's holdings in AMMB, branched out into more aggressive ventures, such as property development and the financing of risky stock market-related corporate transactions.

The change in business strategies that Azman pursued led to a major makeover in AmBank's clientele. From the dozens of state-owned corporations and government agencies that AmBank helped structure bond issues and syndicated loans, the financial house that Azman built shifted its focus. It trained its sights on the lucrative but risky businesses of hire-purchase financing, share trading, and the financing of small- and medium-sized businesses that wanted to list on the country's bullish stock market.

Tragedy struck in the summer of 1997 when regional currencies swooned. Azman, along with dozens of other Malaysia's top corporate tycoons, found themselves stranded in a collapsing stock market. Shares of their listed entities nose-dived overnight—having enjoyed somewhat unrealistic valuations during the boom times—causing loans that were collateralized by stockholdings to turn toxic in the books of financial institutions.

Unlike other Malaysian businessmen who were forced to pay dearly in the aftermath of the crisis, Azman had one ace up his sleeve. He turned to the Mahathir government of the time, and tapped into the emotive issue of race in Malaysia. Azman pleaded with the government that, without some form of a bailout, the Arab Malaysian brand would fall into non-Malay hands. The gambit worked. Assistance flowed in quickly in the shape of a policy initiative to consolidate the country's crowded financial sector—at one point housing fifty-four concerns—into fewer than ten groups that would come under so-called anchor banks. AmBank easily secured the coveted anchor bank status that ensured Azman's survival. The banking group, like much of the rest of corporate Malaysia, recovered on the back of the country's economic rebound and, in May 2007, the Australia and New Zealand Banking Group Ltd, or ANZ, acquired a 24 per cent interest in Azman's banking interests held under AMMB.

The AmBank investment was part of ANZ's push to stamp a presence across nearly thirty markets worldwide. Little did ANZ know that the Malaysian investment would give it so much more: association with a global financial scandal that would become shorthand for corruption, deceit, and national plundering on the widest ever scale in history.

Barely two months after ANZ and AmBank finalized their joint venture, Low tapped on Tang Kee Chee to help him raise funding for the takeover of two mildly profitable construction-based companies that were listed on the Malaysian stock exchange, Putrajaya Perdana and Loh & Loh Corporation.

Tang, or Casey Tang as he presented himself to the local business community, was a known freelance broker and

corporate fixer, who introduced potential .corporate clients to financial institutions. He particularly enjoyed very close relations with senior executives at AmInvestment Bank, AmBank's dealmaking and stockbroking division.

In late July 2007, Low and Tang presented Project Concrete to representatives from AmBank at the Ritz Carlton Hotel in downtown Kuala Lumpur, to seek funding proposals for the corporate takeovers. The Project Concrete document that Low disclosed to the bankers featured the strong political connections and financial muscle the Wynton Group and ADKMIC possessed. It depicted how the private companies were on the cusp of securing contracts for road-building and water-related projects, and entering into partnership with state-owned sovereign fund Khazanah Nasional, the said partnership to jointly develop a multibillion ringgit real estate project in southern Johor state. The two publicly listed entities had been identified as corporate vehicles for the new ventures.

AmBank executives, taken up by Low's aggressive pitch, were already imagining the huge fees they could rake in, advising on the takeover of the two companies, which was surely to lead to more corporate finance work that would in turn result in higher year-end bonuses. Between August and November of 2007, AmBank provided Low's investment vehicles with total funding of MYR 453 million (roughly USD 135 million at the prevailing exchange rates) for the takeover of Putrajaya Perdana and Loh & Loh. It did not matter that the rotund newbie to corporate Malaysia had no credit history whatsoever with the local financial sector or anywhere else.

Low was just getting warmed up.

In mid-2008, Low and his financial advisors embarked on a new corporate exercise. Using another private entity called Majestic Masterpiece, which was ultimately owned by ADKMIC, it trained its sights on UBG, which was sitting on a pile of cash after the sale of its stake in RHB Bank to pension fund EPF. The underlying assets for the UBG takeover were Putrajaya Perdana and Loh & Loh. That deal, which saw UBG acquire the two listed entities through the issues of new shares to Majestic Masterpiece, was financed entirely by a MYR 716 million term loan from AmBank. Bankers familiar with the deal said that the quick flips of Putrajaya Perdana and Loh & Loh earned Low and ADKMIC a profit of nearly MYR 150 million. But this nifty piece of financial engineering should have raised a number of red flags. For starters, the private concerns, or special purpose vehicles (SPVs), were ultimately owned by Low and ADKMIC. All shared the same registered corporate address, and the flips of the same underlying assets (Putrajaya Perdana and Loh & Loh) were designed to facilitate the evergreening of funding facilities. Simply put, an existing financial arrangement was settled with a fresh financing scheme over a longer period.

Related-party transactions are typically frowned upon by regulators, but it would be a pattern that Low would replicate in the coming years with AmBank. Why did AmBank go along with the schemes? The suspicion was always that kickbacks flowed to bankers who facilitated these deals. There was also the promise of the deal of all deals.

6

Project Tiara 2009

Tensions were running high among Najib's core group of advisors and political operatives in late March.

A high-stakes power play in ruling UMNO had just brought an end to Badawi's nearly six-year reign as party president, and the prime ministership that traditionally came with the party position. Najib, who played a key behind-the-scenes role in the ousting of his former boss, had taken over the party presidency. But the appointment letter from the national palace for his swearing-in as the new prime minister before the King was being delayed. What was supposed to be a formality was starting to lurch sideways.

Rumours began to swirl that the monarch, Sultan Mizan Zainal Abidin, from the royal house of the north-eastern Terengganu state, was having second thoughts. The presumptive prime minister was embroiled in a shocking crime that was apparently linked to a financial scandal—the

gruesome killing of a Mongolian woman and millions of dollars in kickbacks from Malaysia's submarine purchases. There was another reason for Najib's acute anxiety over this royal house. Only a year earlier, Sultan Mizan had publicly opposed the UMNO nominee for the post of chief minister in his state and insisted that the party submit other potential candidates for him to consider. It was unprecedented in Malaysian politics because the head of state traditionally acted on the advice of the prime minister, under the country's unique constitutional monarchy that was ensconced in its parliamentary system. A looming constitutional crisis was only averted after UMNO leaders submitted a fresh name that was acceptable to the palace.

The Najib camp did not have anyone to effectively represent its interests to the palace. That was until Low stepped up.

Nizam, Low's business partner in Wynton, had introduced the young businessman to his elder brother, Najib, months earlier. Najib, the deputy prime minister, was taken up by the businessman's Middle East connections, especially his ties to members of Arab royal households.

When Low got wind of the tizzy in the Najib camp over the King's apparent reluctance to sign the all-important instrument of appointment, he offered to intervene. Low was well placed. First, he had recruited Sultan Mizan's sister, Tengku Rahimah Mahmud Billal Shah, as a shareholder to several shell companies used in the UBG takeover. Second, Low had also become close to the King himself. He had been appointed as economic advisor to the Terengganu palace and was working to establish a state-owned sovereign wealth fund for Sultan Mizan.

Within days of Low's offer to help, Najib received his appointment letter. It isn't clear whether Low had anything to do with it, but Najib and his domineering wife, Rosmah Mansor, nevertheless assigned him all credit. And to show their gratitude, Low was given a seat at the main table.

The timing could not have been more fortuitous for Low. Three months earlier, Low and his sidekick Tang had approached AmBank with the single largest deal the bank had even seen—a proposal for a multibillion ringgit issue of bonds, guaranteed directly by the federal government. Additional collateral was provided by the resource-rich Terengganu state, in the form of annual oil and gas royalties paid by national oil corporation Petronas, the country's only Fortune 500 listing.

The plan to establish the state sovereign fund was pitched to AmBank as an initiative first mooted by Sultan Mizan. It had been raised at a cabinet meeting in mid-December 2008, while Abdullah was still prime minister, and given initial approval. In late February 2009, the Terengganu Investment Authority (TIA) was incorporated under what was dubbed within AmBank as Project Tiara. But the scheme quickly came up against some spirited opposition from Terengganu state government officials, who were concerned about potential defaults should TIA not be able to generate returns to meet annual interest payments on the bonds. Sultan Mizan was also starting to get cold feet.

Low then turned to Najib, who quickly warmed to the entrepreneur's idea. And why not? Only four years earlier, Najib, who was then both deputy prime minister and defence minister, had been in talks with the UK's BAE Systems Plc. The UK entity had established close relations with Najib's office, and was in discussions over an arms deal that called for

the Malaysian government to commit part of the country's gold reserves to help finance the purchase of warships and other defence equipment valued at roughly GBP 1 billion, or about USD 1.8 billion (MYR 6.84 billion) at prevailing exchange rates.

The proposal, initiated by BAE and excitedly welcomed by Najib at the time, called for the British defence contractor to arrange funding for the arms purchases with a loan secured by gold certificates issued by the Malaysian government.

The BAE plan was compelling on several fronts. For starters, it was notable for its innovation, just when the government was pushing to cut its budget deficit and shy away from big-ticket contracts. BAE's use of the country's gold reserves as security for the defence purchases represented a novel way to secure funding at very low rates, which at the time was estimated at less than 1 per cent. Malaysia's financial reserves, represented by national gold and foreign exchange holdings at the time, stood at roughly USD 66 billion.

A typical economic measure applied for reserves in this case was that Malaysia had enough to finance eight months of retained imports. The BAE proposal called for committing only 2.8 per cent of the total national reserves—a very achievable proposition.

But the scheme quickly found detractors after the plan was exposed by my reporting in *The Asian Wall Street Journal* in early May 2005. Pledging the national reserves as collateral for a commercial deal had never been done before. What's more, Malaysia had already been badly singed, in the early 90s, when Mahathir sanctioned Negara to commit the country's then bountiful foreign reserves to trade aggressively in international foreign exchange markets, a foray that had ended in disaster.

There was also a strong political dimension to the opposition. Najib was widely considered an UMNO warlord because of the political slush fund he had amassed as defence minister under procurement deals that were opaque and often laden with kickbacks. If the deal was approved, Najib, who was already eyeing to unseat Badawi, would be unstoppable.

As the newly appointed PM and finance minister in April 2009, Najib's immediate challenge was to solidify his control over UMNO, which could only be achieved by cranking-up the flow of patronage and bringing UMNO's growing cast of warlords under his command. Low's Project Tiara suited Najib because the bonds needed a government guarantee that only he could provide. There was no need to consult any other government regulatory agency. Najib, with Low's help, had sowed the seeds for his slush fund, which was presented to Malaysians and the investing public as a strategic sovereign fund that would invest in energy assets overseas.

By mid-April 2009, word began to circulate in Malaysia's clubby banking fraternity that AmBank had secured the sole mandate as principal advisor and lead arranger for the issue of a thirty-year Islamic bond paper, guaranteed by the government, and projected to raise a minimum of MYR 5 billion (roughly USD 1.5 billion at the time).

State-controlled CIMB financial group, the country's second largest lender, headed by Najib's younger brother, Nazir Razak, wanted a piece of the action. Nazir told a visitor to his office at the time that he had spoken to his brother about getting CIMB, which was already regarded as one of the country's most deal-driven financial houses, to jointly drive the bond issue with AmBank. But Najib rebuffed his overtures. The elder brother bluntly noted that 'CIMB already had enough on its plate'.

Bond markets are considered staid and are not widely followed by the average investor, who is typically attracted by equities because of the potential for a higher return. But for long-term investors, such as large pension funds and insurance companies, bonds are preferred because they provide a stable return. Simply put, bonds are IOUs issued by governments and corporations; they carry a fixed interest rate over a certain period of time; and the principal is paid back in full when the issue matures.

Then there are investment-grade bonds and high-yield issues.

'Investment grade' is typically assigned to governments and financially sound entities because they have a higher credit rating and pay a lower interest rate due to the low risk of default.

High-yield means the issuer has a lower credit rating and is forced to pay a higher interest rate in exchange for the greater likelihood of default.

Apart from the coupon rate, which represents the annual interest payment, another important matrix to consider is the yield-to-maturity. The YTM, as it is commonly referred to by market players, is the average rate of return the investor would receive over the bond's lifetime.

From the very start, the proposed TIA bond issue was a cause for uneasiness within AmBank, particularly the question of whether the financial institution would be able to absorb a huge bond issue that carried such a long tenure. It was unprecedented for AmBank. Several members of its senior management had suggested that the bank bring on other local financial institutions to play the role of co-lead advisor and arranger, to help spread the risk of underwriting the huge bond issue.

Project Tiara, however, could not afford the prying eyes of another lender and, to head off concerns, Low's trusted acolytes in the bank argued otherwise, stressing that AmBank's balance sheet was strong enough for the financial institution to go solo. Why share the potential millions of dollars in fees, that would in turn translate to hefty year-end bonuses?

In reality, the naysayers to the TIA plan were few. Many in AmBank's top management had been seduced by the promise of financial reward from Project Tiara and the other stream of deals Low was promising. In order to protect and manipulate the whole scheme, only a select few would be directly involved in the project, and Low kept the circle tight.

Apart from his long-time right-hand man, Tang, Low's external team included:

- Goldman Sachs banker Roger Ng, who would later become one of the central players in this massive global swindle. Ng has been found guilty of stealing billions of dollars from the 1MDB fund after a lengthy court case fought by US state prosecutors.
- Kee Kok Thiam, who worked directly for the Wynton Group.

The main cohorts at AmBank were:

- Teng Chean Choy, who headed the treasury and markets division and drove all deals from within;
- Chan Wan Seong and Joanna Yu, the two senior personal relationship bankers to Low; and
- Cheah Tek Kuang, AmBank's managing director.

Cheah was a crucial player. As a senior member of the bank's top management, Cheah was able to steer the Low-related deals over the hoops posed by the bank's compliance and audit committees. Cheah also enjoyed close relations with two other very important players in the Malaysian government: Negara governor, Zeti, and Nor Mohamed, the one-time rogue currency trader who successfully rehabilitated himself to hold the position of special functions economic minister in Najib's Prime Minister's Department.

Cheah, Zeti, and Nor Mohamed were also all members of the Economics faculty at the University of Malaya.

Two elements are critical in a bond swindle.

The first is securing the right coupon and the YTM rate.

In mid-April 2009, Jonathan Manifold, the head of risk management at AmBank, emailed the bank's top management overseeing the planned TIA scheme to say he estimated the fair market YTM for the TIA bond issues at 4.72 per cent, based on the 4.72 per cent yield US Treasuries were fetching at the time, and by assigning a so-called 25 basis points spread. This would have roughly been the rate for any typical bond issue guaranteed by the Malaysian government.

But the TIA bond was a lot more. It was an elaborate exercise in fraud to siphon money and to use it to create a political slush fund for Najib. The rate Manifold had recommended would have been devastating for Project Tiara.

This was a huge problem. A higher coupon would be crucially beneficial for the plan to succeed. Never mind that the Malaysian taxpayer would have to pay a high annual rate of interest for the thirty-year bond. The overriding objective was to create conditions that would provide all the latitude

for the schemers to structure the deal in ways that would allow them to squeeze money up front.

Manifold's all-important email on the recommended rate for the TIA bonds quickly disappeared into the ether. AmBank's Teng and Chan began arguing that the TIA bond proposal was far from being a typical government-backed bond issue.

Further, Teng and Chan had personally lined up four foreign parties that had expressed a keen interest in underwriting the bonds. The only notable name in the list was the BNP Paribas chapter based out of Singapore. The other three were:

- Thailand-based Adkinson Securities, a listed financial outfit that was later renamed Country Group Securities, and which was controlled by the Taechaubol family;
- Little known Shikumen Capital Management Ltd, which was incorporated in the Cayman Islands and had operations in Hong Kong; and
- Aktis Capital Singapore, a financial advisory and fund management outfit headed by banker Cheah Teik Seng, who worked in the Malaysian Finance Ministry and was known to be close to Nor Mohamed.

Now, the second element for the swindle would kick in—the mode of issue for the bonds. Depending on the nature of the bonds issues and arrangers, financial advisors would suggest one of three routes—a Private Placement, a Book Building exercise, or a Bought Deal. A Private Placement by a little-known company known as TIA was likely to face some hurdles. The most obvious track would be Book

Building, simply because the bonds would be in keen demand to investors as the papers carried a government guarantee. All AmBank had to do was to underwrite the amount that investors would not have taken up. But there was no money to be made in these two approaches. Low and his team of schemers then decided to cherry-pick elements from all three modes of issue to create a financial structure that would enable them to extract as much as possible from the bond issue upfront.

Project Tiara would apply a Bought Deal, which is usually utilized for cases involving high-yield papers, where the issuer's credit standing is weak and a higher coupon is required to attract investors.

Both Teng and Chan drove the proposed bond issue, taking regular instructions from Low, who also had TIA's then chief executive officer, Shahrol Azral Halmi, on his side.

The following reconstruction of events, based on internal AmBank documents and interviews, show that the three men put up an impressive charade to pull off this multibillion-ringgit scam.

Teng and Chan informed their AmBank bosses in an internal memo in mid-May 2009 that BNP Paribas, the only internationally recognizable party in the three-member panel of sub-underwriters, had pulled out from the proposed bond deal because the French banking giant's position was to 'focus on short term paper and therefore their participation is considered remote'.[1]

---

[1] The construction of these developments and events are based on interviews with AmBank executives and a review of internal AmBank documents and emails.

Little-known Shikumen would also drop out, leaving Thailand's Country Group Securities (CGS) and Singapore's Aktis Capital as the remaining participants.

The path was now laid for Low and his AmBank accomplices to move to the next level by stage-managing elaborate negotiations over the coupon and YTM rates, through memos and correspondences to parties wanting participation in the deal. After several days of sham haggling, all parties decided that the TIA bonds would be issued at a coupon rate of 5.75 per cent and a YTM of 6.67 per cent annually. All of this was approved by Shahrol, the then CEO at TIA.

There was another element in the deal that all parties agreed to: The MYR 5 billion bonds would be issued with a 13 per cent discount on its face value for the sub-underwriters—Country Group Securities would take up MYR 3.8 billion, Aktis was in for MYR 700 million, and the remaining MYR 500 million was to be subscribed by AmBank.

The final pieces of this elaborate financial swindle were to appoint AmBank as the placement agent and to identify secondary investors that would take up these respective allocations.

Game on!

On 27 May 2009, two days before issuance of the MYR 5 billion thirty-year tenure TIA bonds, later to be renamed 1Malaysia Development Bhd (1MDB), AmBank easily secured a full subscription of the bonds on behalf of the sub-underwriters without any discount. The buyers were Malaysian pension funds, foreign and local insurance companies, and local fund managers, all of whom would have

picked up these papers anyway had the investment products been offered to them in the first place.

In just two months, from the inception of the deal to the placement date, Country Group Securities and Aktis made a financial killing without any financial outlay.

Aktis received MYR 74.6 million (roughly USD 21.2 million) into its United Overseas Bank (UOB) in Singapore within hours of the full subscription of the bonds.

The payment arrangements for Country Securities Group of MYR 404.6 million (USD 114.7 million) was more peculiar. On 28 May, the Thai financial group dispatched a letter addressed exclusively to AmBank's Teng, requesting him to make a payment of MYR 4.6 million (USD 1.3 million) into its Siam Commercial Bank account in Bangkok. The remainder of MYR 400 million (USD 113.4 million) was payable to a previously undisclosed 'transaction partner', ACME Time Ltd, a BVI-incorporated concern. Teng was told to credit the amount into ACME's account in RBS Coutts Singapore. ACME Time was unknown to most in the bank. But subsequent reviews by AmBank's own internal auditors would later reveal that the option agreement between CSG and ACME Time was executed by Eric Tan, a known associate of Low's.

The complicity of the top management of AmBank in siphoning the proceeds of the TIA bond issue may be difficult to prove. But the lapses that allowed for this to happen are staggering. Subsequent audit reviews revealed that payment instructions from Aktis Capital, CSG, and ACME Time, which furnished details of their respective bank accounts, were addressed to a person with the email handle of 'Lancy Kwan'. AmBank's Human Resource Department would later confirm that there was no employee with that name.

This much is hard to deny: The way the deal was structured shows clear possible collusion between Low, TIA's CEO of the time, Shahrol, and the AmBank executives, primarily Teng and Chan. Said structure enabled CSG, ACME Time, and Aktis to benefit from the steep discount and subsequent flip. AmBank had no previous dealing with all three parties.

An AmBank internal audit report prepared for the financial institution's governance committee some six years later, in May 2015, stated that the senior management, including managing director Cheah, as well as Kok Tuck Cheong and Pushpa Rajadurai (respectively, managing director and executive director of the bank's advisory division), had 'no total re-collection' of the details of the bond issue 'in terms of the pricing, engagement of the sub-underwriters and the placement' of the bonds.

'All seemed to suggest that the main person central to the issuance and identifying the sub-underwriters was Teng,' referring to AmBank's head of treasury. The report further added that the internal audit team was 'unable to confirm how the off-shore sub-underwriters were sourced or the criteria used in the selection of the sub-underwriters for consideration, as the underlying documents and work papers related to the matter kept by Teng' were not made available and the team had no opportunity to interview him. But the internal audit report does state 'that based on meetings and interviews with senior management and the relationship managers, it was suspected that the names could have been possibly provided to Teng by the issuer (TIA)', a codeword for Low.

More intriguing was the glaring failure of Malaysia's central bank, Negara, to investigate suspicious transactions, especially the flow of funds out of the Malaysian banking system to the sub-underwriters in Singapore and Thailand.

Low had that end covered. Not only was he regularly schmoozing with governor Zeti's husband, Ayman, he was also a regular guest at their home most weekends. Low recalls how he would bring expensive white wines, which Ayman was particularly partial to, and Zeti herself would cook spaghetti meals for him. 'I very much enjoyed those afternoons,' Low remembers.

7

Going Rogue

Red flags should have also been raised by the wide cast of professional outfits involved in the TIA bond issue. Apart from Goldman Sachs, the other professional entities involved in Project Tiara included Boston Consulting Group; JPMorgan; accounting firm KPMG; two Malaysian law firms, Kadir Andri & Partners and Shearn Delamore & Co, both high-street practices; and Singapore-based Allen & Overy Shook Lin & Bok. But Low made it clear to all the professionals that this was a deal personally backed by PM Najib and there were not going to be any obstacles from Negara. One lawyer who was involved in Project Tiara acknowledged to me much later: 'At all times all of us skated very close to the line and very often we crossed it. All because we were told that the government and Najib wanted this done.'

For his part, Najib, who was prime minister and finance minister, did not want any direct connection with the bond issue. He simply nudged the deal along with the strong backing of the finance ministry. Apart from the government guarantee for the MYR 5 billion bond that was issued on

15 May 2009, the stamp of the prime minister and finance minister did not appear on paper. But a near disaster forced Najib into the open just a week after the federal government guarantee was issued.

The head of the Terengganu royal household, Sultan Mizan, who was also Malaysia's king at the time, suddenly turned sour on the bond plan by the state-owned TIA and ordered the immediate suspension of the issue, barely a week after the Najib government had agreed to fully guarantee the entire financial exercise. A letter dated 22 May and signed by the King's sister, Tengku Rahimah, the newly appointed director to the TIA board, was dispatched to AmBank. The letter carried instructions to suspend all matters related to the bond issue. It also served as a notification that TIA's often mercurial CEO, Shahrol, had been suspended with immediate effect and stripped of all executive powers. It was a Friday, the bond issue was now dead, and Najib had to step in.

The events to follow show that both Low and Najib were joined at the hip and that Project Tiara clearly had all the PM's blessings.

- Over the weekend, Najib instructs Low and Shahrol to proceed as planned. He will personally handle the situation with the Terengganu royal household.
- On Monday, 25 May 2009, Shahrol, who has already been stripped of all executive powers in TIA, issues a letter to AmBank to proceed immediately with the bond issue.
- Two days later, Najib is granted an audience with Sultan Mizan and both agree that the bond issue will be suspended pending the appointment of

an oversight committee in TIA to evaluate the bond issue.

- About the same time as the meeting at the Royal Chulan Palace in Kuala Lumpur, AmBank executives push ahead with the bond issue and, surprisingly, achieve a full subscription of the bonds on behalf of the sub-underwriters, Country Securities Group, and Aktis Capital.
- That same day, 27 May 2009, at the federal government's weekly cabinet meeting, Najib informs his ministers that he has had an audience with Sultan Mizan; he gives the impression that the bond issue is on track.
- The bond issue is completed on 29 May and promptly published on the official website, called Bond Info Hub, which is supervised by the central bank; the news on Bond Info Hub catches the Terengganu state government by surprise.
- The state administration immediately and officially states its displeasure in letters to the Najib government and AmBank. The state government accuses AmBank of corruption for proceeding with the issue.
- To paper over all these cracks in the bond issue, which are fraudulent and illegal, Najib presents a new narrative to his cabinet colleagues in the weekly meeting of early June, stating that certain 'unauthorised acts had culminated in the illegal issue of the TIA bonds'.
- He immediately suggests remedial actions, including the takeover of TIA by the federal government and

the assumption of all liabilities from the issuance of the bonds.

- The government also decides that the matter need not be placed before parliament, and that the country's auditor-general does not have to review the company's affair because, as a private limited entity, TIA's finances are to be audited by private accounting firm Ernst & Young. An entire illegal fundraising becomes kosher.
- In the third week of September 2009, the entire process of transforming TIA into a federal government entity is completed. The company has now morphed into 1Malaysia Development Berhad, with MYR 4.39 billion in the kitty. Of this amount, MYR 2.5 billion is deposited into the company account at RHB Bank, and the remaining MYR 1.89 billion remains in AmBank, for payments to Country Securities and Aktis Capital from the original bond proceeds.

Najib's direct intervention to salvage the bond issue was a vivid display of the serious wasta Low was packing. It also gave Low the confidence that there was no financial scheme too audacious to attempt. After squeezing over MYR 600 million upfront from the bond issue, Low quickly set his eyes on the MYR 4.39 billion in the kitty, and immediately began working on a new financial structure.

For any scheme to fly, Low needed to stick very close to TIA's official remit of seeking investments in energy assets overseas through joint ventures, particularly with cash-flushed Middle Eastern entities.

Faraway Turkmenistan, in Central Asia, fitted the bill nicely. Ranked among the top ten gas producers globally, Turkmenistan sits strategically in a hugely conflicted area dominated by Russia and contested by the likes of the US, Europe, and China, all clamouring for access to its vast gas fields. In mid-2009, the frenzied race for a piece of the action produced unlikely bedfellows. One such pairing was a joint venture between Merhav, an Israeli conglomerate run by a former intelligence officer from the storied foreign intelligence service Mossad, and PetroSaudi International of Saudi Arabia, a company owned by the son of the then Saudi king, Abdullah bin Abdulaziz.

Saudi Arabia's laid-back Prince Turki Abdullah controlled PetroSaudi with his business partner, Tarek Obaid. Both Arab businessmen were known to Low, and PetroSaudi appeared as an ideal vehicle to set the scam in motion. Never mind that the Riyadh-incorporated PetroSaudi had negligible revenue to show after being in business for more than four years, and that it was by all means a dormant corporate entity. Its ostensible presence in resource-rich Turkmenistan provided a major opportunity for financial tricksters like Low. Their modus operandi was to wrap up so-called assets in remote regions, where credible information is difficult to come by, and throw in fancy valuation reports by experts of some repute.

PetroSaudi was presented to the 1MDB board and Najib as a known international player in the oil and gas business with close ties to the Saudi royal family. The company had secured exploration rights in Turkmenistan and Argentina, with proven reserves valued at close to USD 3 billion, if not more, and the entity was keen to take on partners. Low

further claimed that he had convinced the Saudis to enter into a joint venture with 1MDB as part of the Najib government's initiative to foster closer diplomatic and economic ties with the Arab kingdom.

Najib gave the PetroSaudi deal the green light pending a full approval by the newly constituted board of 1MDB that was now wholly owned by the government entity called Minister of Finance Inc. Better known as MOF Inc., this entity is a corporate body that was established under legislation at the time of independence in 1957 to allow the government to enter into contracts, purchases, and other activities, such as investment holding.

The board of 1MDB was given a position paper on the investment in the third week of September 2009, which called for the setting up of a new joint venture entity called 1MDB PetroSaudi International in the Cayman Islands.

The board was also informed that 1MDB's management had commissioned Edward Lewis Morse, a former official of the US State Department's energy division, to carry out a valuation of the PetroSaudi assets. As an energy analyst and gun-for-hire valuation consultant who had had a stint with Lehman Brothers, Morse only provided an economic valuation of the oil contained in the fields. Nothing was raised about the fact that the oil fields in the Caspian Sea would be tough to exploit because of the ongoing territorial dispute between Turkmenistan and Azerbaijan.

The Morse report was rosy, valuing the oil assets at USD 2.7 billion. On 29 September 2009, the joint venture agreement was signed, with 1MDB committing a USD 1 billion investment to the deal in return for a 40 per cent

interest; the entity was incorporated in the Cayman Islands and named 1MDB PetroSaudi International.

The following day, 30 September 2009, Zeti, as central bank governor, would make that fateful appearance at the foreign exchange trading floor at Negara headquarters in downtown KL and smooth over the transfer of the 1MDB monies by the Malaysian-based operations of Deutsche Bank.

In just over a week, 1MDB had committed nearly 80 per cent of the funds raised from the bond issue into one single investment.

In reality, the biggest swindle in Malaysian history had just been committed through an elaborate scheme of financial chicanery that was bundled together during the last two weeks of September. It involved creating a corporate debt using legal fiction that was disguised through equity cross-holdings in offshore jurisdictions (Cayman Islands, British Virgin Islands, Jersey, and Panama), which made it impossible to conduct any robust due diligence to determine either the value of the assets, if any, or to determine the legal ownership.

What is more remarkable is the short space of time in which this heist was hatched. The position paper that was presented to the 1MDB board hid all the violations that took place.

Here is a distilled reconstruction of how the theft played out.

On 29 Sept 2009, the same day the joint venture agreement was signed by both PetroSaudi and 1MDB, the top management of both companies signed a so-called 'Letter of Agreement' to amend the key elements of the new pact,

which would significantly alter the flow of funds from the Malaysian sovereign entity.

The amendment called to split the USD 1 billion payment from 1MDB for its 40 per cent interest. Only USD 300 million would be paid into the new joint venture entity's account at JPMorgan Bank. The remainder was to be directly paid by 1MDB itself into an account nominated by a PetroSaudi concern incorporated in Cayman Islands, which had created assets through legal deceit using the highly dubious oil and gas assets in Turkmenistan and Argentina.

While 1MDB was a principal signatory in the joint venture, Riyadh-based PetroSaudi was not. The company hid behind a web of companies in the four offshore jurisdictions with one concern owning the assets that had been valued at USD 2.7 billion.

All these corporate structures were established just days before 1MDB signed the joint venture and transferred the USD 1 billion for its 40 per cent interest. Almost immediately after the money arrived from 1MDB, the new joint venture settled the debt owed by transferring USD 700 million to a third-party entity known as Good Star Ltd, which held an account in RBS Coutts Bank Ltd. Behind the web of bearer shares hid the company's true ownership—Good Star, and Low was Good Star.

8

The Swindle Grows 2010

By early 2010, Malaysia's political troubles had calmed markedly, largely because Najib moved quickly to placate the prickly and combative Mahathir, who had anointed himself as the grand overseer of all matters Malaysian. Najib's push for the return of mega-projects, fashioned along Mahathir's dubious brand of command capitalism, endeared him to the eighty-five-year-old man, who was showing no signs of slowing down. Even the 1MDB initiative, still fuzzy to observers at that time, won quiet praise from Mahathir, who told associates that the creation of a sovereign fund was a novel way to finance and promote development through foreign investment and partnerships, both of which would have typically been caught up with bureaucratic and parliamentary hurdles had the government relied on traditional approaches.

It was in sharp contrast to Mahathir's treatment of Najib's predecessor, Badawi. Mahathir's open and relentless attacks against Badawi, who was his successor, led many

of Malaysia's business elite to shy away from Abdullah's team of advisors, which included former consulting executives led by his son, Kamaluddin; the Oxford-trained son-in-law, Khairy; and a gaggle of mediocre businessmen and corporate fixers. At best, they were shown token support by the Mahathir cronies. They were seen as fixers who were close to Badawi, with extended experience in finance-related consultancy and brokerage arrangements that would be of assistance to the government. Nothing really big.

Najib, however, was different. The tacit endorsement for the Najib administration by Mahathir had a weighty impact on Malaysia Inc., the conglomerate of crony businessmen whose domination of strategic sectors of the Malaysian economy came via the awards they received to privatize essential services. These services ranged from the management of ports, mobile telecommunication operations, power generation, and other infrastructure-related ventures, all of which had long concession periods that guaranteed untold profits. The cronies reasoned that the Najib-led government had longevity with Mahathir's tacit backing, which meant they needed to build ties with influence-peddlers in Najib's inner circle so they may find favour with the government when seeking extensions on soon-to-end concession deals and approvals for expansion plans. Now, to find the go-to person.

Low soon became that person. His closeness to Najib's children and, more importantly, the fondness for Low held by the prime minister's hot-tempered and hugely influential wife, Rosmah, were key elements to his rise. Rosmah was quick with a sharp rebuke when lesser business gophers whined about the negative publicity Low was drawing with his flashy lifestyle abroad, hosting lavish parties with celebrities such as

Leonardo DiCaprio, Alicia Keys, Megan Fox, Miranda Kerr, and Paris Hilton. Najib was always full of praise for Low. He often told his senior civil servants that all he had to do was to ponder something aloud and Low would get the ball rolling to deliver.

During a brief Kuwait layover to refuel the Malaysian government's official jet, enroute to Kuala Lumpur after an official visit to France, Najib was with his ambassador in the Gulf state. The prime minister wondered about the chances of meeting with his Kuwaiti counterpart. Najib was told the Kuwaitis were sticklers for protocol and that it would be difficult. Word somehow reached Low, who was not on the trip but clearly had aides who kept him in the know and on the ball. Shortly after the jet took off from Kuwait International Airport, some 16 kilometres from Kuwait City, the pilot received instructions to turn the plane around because the meeting had been secured. It was all Low's doing and Najib and Rosmah never got tired of recounting this episode in private settings, when waxing lyrical about their unlikely young fixer's resourcefulness.

What separated Low from businessmen and operatives claiming to have a seat at the kitchen cabinet was the fact that he had devised a neat 1MDB slush fund that was central to Najib consolidating his grip over the ruling UMNO party. The UMNO that Najib inherited from his predecessor was riddled with factions and the party was still smarting from the electoral setbacks of the 2008 general election. But with access to the stockpile of cash raised from the 1MDB bond issue, Najib quickly bought the loyalty of a majority of UMNO warlords with regular cash payouts. Najib's strategy of 'cash is king'—a phrase he invoked many times in private

conversations with his close advisors, and which he would later tout publicly—worked well in UMNO, too well in fact. Soon Najib realized that the handouts could not stop. The UMNO chieftains had become hooked and the only way to keep them in line was to provide them with that constant fix.

The creation of the 1MDB slush fund also made Najib independent of the political-crony economic model Mahathir had put in place during his first stint as prime minister, which began in 1981 and lasted twenty-two years.

In the opaque world of Mahathir's once vaunted and now beleaguered privatization schemes, a select group of businessmen and corporate groups were awarded exclusive rights to build and operate a range of public works projects. They then became major providers of funds for the UMNO-led coalition—itself in power since independence in 1957—and most of them were aligned to the Mahathir circle of influence. With the political donations came more requests for favours in the form of government contracts.

With 1MDB, however, Najib was beholden to no party or group. But it also meant that Low, whose expertise was central in keeping the slush fund firing on all cylinders, had become crucial to Najib's political longevity.

The first hurdle to keeping 1MDB as a going concern emerged in mid-2010. 1MDB, which had committed nearly 80 per cent of the monies raised from the September 2009 bond issue, was running out of funds and needed to raise fresh loans to deal with looming annual interest payments to bondholders and to finance its own operations. But, turning to the banks without being able to show a kosher set of

financial accounts, even for a government-owned entity, was a non-starter.

Like in any scam, window-dressing the accounts is always a good starting point. Low and 1MDB's top brass decided to apply some creative accounting to paper over the fraud that had siphoned more than USD 700 million of the funds raised from the bond issue, so as to turn the fictional debt with PetroSaudi into a new financial fairy tale.

In its maiden annual report for the financial year ending 31 March 2010, 1MDB disclosed that it had disposed of its equity holdings in the joint venture with PetroSaudi—entered into the previous September—and harvested roughly USD 200 million profit from the divestment. That transaction, involving the fund's only investment, allowed 1MDB to register a pre-tax profit of just over USD 110 million for its first year in business, which Najib and gang quickly trumpeted in public to show that the new sovereign fund was doing well. In fact, the set of annual accounts was nothing more than a cheat-sheet. The divestment of the equity interest in the joint venture company was a cashless transaction. After investing USD 1 billion in the venture, the Malaysian state-owned fund accepted an eleven-year repayment scheme structured along the line of an Islamic bond, which included commitments from a BVI-incorporated entity.

With the books now cooked, 1MDB wasted no time to raise more borrowings. In September 2010, AmBank and Standard Chartered Bank in Malaysia together approved a MYR 2.5 billion (about USD 782 million at the prevailing exchange rate) syndicated term loan for 1MDB that was ostensibly meant to finance investments in an unnamed

public-listed business in Europe, and strategic economic sectors domestically. In fact, it was a cover for more financial shenanigans. Between early September 2010 and mid-May 2011, the 1MDB management team, led by TIA's Shahrol, executed three drawdowns on the freshly raised syndicated term loan. The grounds behind the request for the release of funds were bogus, and it should have been flagged by Malaysia's central bank, Negara. Here is what happened:

- In the second week of September 2010, shortly after the syndicated term loan was approved, Shahrol requested a drawdown of USD 500 million (about MYR 1.6 billion at that time) to finance the subscription of a tranche of Islamic bonds overseas. Oddly enough, just two days after the amount was transferred overseas to acquire the bonds, AmBank received USD 260 million on behalf of a private, Malaysian-incorporated company that was proposing to take over several entities related to Low. They were the same entities—Utama Banking Group (UBG), Putrajaya Perdana, and Loh & Loh Corp.—that Low had acquired two years earlier with financing raised by AmBank, as noted in Chapter 4. Auditors from PricewaterhouseCoopers (PwC) would later suggest that reviews of email chains and other correspondence between AmBank and counterparties suggest that the money was from the first drawdown. Low was using 1MDB money as his private piggy bank and certain parties at AmBank were clearly complicit.

- In early March 2011, Shahrol made a request for a second drawdown of MYR 715 million (roughly USD 216 million then) to fund a real estate project in Kuala Lumpur. But the PwC review six years later would discover that roughly MYR 226 million from the second drawdown was transferred to the account of UK-based law firm Shearman & Sterling. That sum financed a Low-related acquisition of a group of companies that owned London's leading hotels, including Claridge's, The Connaught, and The Berkeley.
- Two months after the second drawdown, Shahrol was back again with another request to transfer roughly USD 330 million to the Low-controlled Good Star, which was going into another oil and gas venture with 1MDB and PetroSaudi. It spooked the already uncomfortable bankers at Standard Chartered, which had co-financed the syndicated term loan with AmBank, on grounds that the details of the proposed investment were too 'vague'. But that did not deter the Shahrol-led management. Clearly, Low's Good Star was in need of urgent funding.
- A fresh request was made weeks later for a drawdown amounting to MYR 1.08 billion to help fund another Najib-backed multibillion-ringgit property development called Bandar Malaysia. The drawdown was approved by Standard Chartered and monies transferred to 1MDB's account at AmBank. Shortly after, MYR 1.08 billion was transferred in four separate tranches to the Low-controlled entity—three by AmBank and another amounting to

> USD 110 million by Deutsche Bank. This MYR 1.08 billion, when converted to the greenback, amounted to USD 330 million, which was the same amount of funds originally requested for the Good Star venture. It is unclear if Standard Chartered gave its approval for the offshore transfers.

Low, the 1MDB management, and AmBank were collectively acting in flagrant disregard of banking conventions. Low started by getting funding for his private Malaysian investment from AmBank and embarked on a carousel of financial flips involving the same underlying corporate assets. He went about creating new special-purpose corporate vehicles to take over the same assets with fresh loans from Am Bank that were used to settle previous facilities provided by the bank. When he ran short, he tapped on funds from 1MDB to settle these payments and also for underwriting his other deal overseas. This round-tripping of 1MDB funds and the ever-greening of Low's private loan facilities were central to the 1MDB heist. Between 1MDB's incorporation in March 2009 and 2011, Low's Good Star, a private entity incorporated in Seychelles, was beneficiary to more than USD 1 billion of diverted funds from 1MDB.

9

New Scam 2012

Low's stock with Malaysian PM Najib was at an all-time high. The creation of 1MDB, and its use as a secret slush fund, allowed Najib to both control politics and set the economic agenda without having to rely on powerful vested-interest groups that had long funded political campaigns and successive governments in return for lucrative contracts and concessions of the sort mentioned earlier. Malaysia's business and political elite were also beginning to notice the weighty influence Low wielded, making him one of the most courted personalities in Najib's inner circle. But Malaysia's banking community began to view Low's rise with unease. His debt-load with AmBank, together with the borrowings that 1MDB was securing with the financier's direct involvement, were making other large financial institutions wary of doing business with him and the highly leveraged sovereign fund.

All of this proved particularly gnawing for 1MDB CEO Shahrol, whose relationship with Low was becoming increasingly strained. While Low was receiving all the credit for devising the political slush fund for Najib, Shahrol—a lanky, one-time IT consultant with Accenture who had graduated from Stanford University in the US—had to do all the dirty work, signing off on Low's fraudulent schemes to siphon money from 1MDB. The disquiet over Low's increasingly chequered reputation among bankers quickly reached Shahrol, who was widely regarded as Najib and Low's errand boy at 1MDB. After facilitating the drawdowns from the syndicated term loan provided by AmBank and Standard Chartered in mid-2011, Shahrol began distancing himself from Low, keeping communications to the bare minimum.

The cold-shoulder treatment Low was getting from the 1MDB management bothered him very little. He was still Najib's point man for 1MDB and there were other urgent duties he had to attend to. 1MDB needed a new scheme to raise funding and Low knew that Shahrol did not have the financial wherewithal to come up with a plan. To begin with, the fictional joint venture with PetroSaudi, which allowed for the siphoning of the bulk of the proceeds of the first bond issue, had called for creative accounting. What was needed now was another scheme to be layered over the first one, and this was familiar terrain for Low. Unlike the first scheme, which was premised on a financial charade involving a fictional debt, the new ruse would have to feature tangible assets that delivered strong cash flows to create the environment for another bond issue.

The first quarter of 2012 saw an alignment of the combined interests of Low and Ananda Krishnan, the

Malaysian tycoon who had made international headlines for his role in helping raise funds for the 1985 Live Aid concert in London. Low got wind from his banking contacts that Ananda, widely known for his hard-charging management style, was eyeing a reorganization of his corporate world, which owned controlling stakes in the country's first pay TV operation, Malaysia's only satellite company, power generation, and oil and gas assets.

Making contact with Ananda was no problem for Low. Ananda always placed a huge premium on making the right political connections. Before returning to Malaysia in early 1991 to build on his fortunes under Tanjong Plc, a company listed on both the London and Malaysian stock exchanges, Ananda was one of few Asian businessmen who boasted a network of contacts that gave him access to important people, ranging from heads of government to corporate tycoons and top influence-peddlers in all the main regional economies.

Topping Ananda's list of political connections was Mahathir. Ananda's critics have long maintained Mahathir was instrumental in clearing obstacles to a series of corporate moves that allowed the businessman to finance development of the iconic Twin Towers, skyscrapers that resemble two metallic corn-on-the-cob structures, with minimal financial outlay. The project in the heart of Kuala Lumpur, on a plot of land that had previously been a hundred-acre horse-racing track, was largely financed by national oil corporation Petronas.

To Ananda, Low's creation of 1MDB displayed raw chutzpah that he had not seen in a long time from any budding financier, and he saw it as a quality to be admired. Ananda quickly directed his second-in-command, Augustus

Ralph Marshall—another Malaysian who, like Ananda, is of Sri Lankan stock—to open talks with Low to explore doing business together. High on Ananda's list was whether 1MDB would consider acquiring a company called MEASAT, short for Malaysia East Asia Satellite program, which owned and operated satellites orbiting Asia and Africa.

Ananda argued that assets of strategic importance had to be controlled by the Malaysian government. But Low did not want to saddle 1MDB with a lumbering business that he did not understand. His eyes were instead firmly on Tanjong's power-generation assets. Ananda's group had built an impressive portfolio of such assets with thirteen plants across as many countries. The plants together had a generating capacity of 3.9 gigawatts, which, putting it simply, is enough juice to provide electricity for more than 2.8 million homes. Ananda agreed to part with his power assets on Low's assurance that 1MDB would consider doing a deal on MEASAT after the power sale.

The price tag for the Tanjong energy assets, which included power-generation plants in Malaysia, Bangladesh, Egypt, and the UAE, was pegged at MYR 8 billion (about USD 2.6 billion at the time). The valuations were nothing short of steep, because the power sale concessions the owners were enjoying from the respective utilities in the six countries were soon to expire, though not at the same time. But with 1MDB facing a financial crunch, Low figured that he would agree to the lofty price tag on condition that Ananda's companies would front the first stage of the funding exercise before 1MDB could explore other funding options, including a fresh international bond issue.

The main bugbear facing the deal was how to come up with the equity portion of the transaction before financial institutions would be ready to lend more funds to bankroll the acquisition. The cash in 1MDB's books was running low, and the sovereign fund did not own an asset that could be liquidated in order to finance the deal.

There were other issues. 1MDB's existing lenders had imposed strict covenants that blocked the sovereign fund from leveraging itself further. At the same time, the Najib government was reluctant to provide any fresh guarantees to the state-controlled firm, which was already saddled with close to MYR 6.8 billion in debt. To win favour with Najib, and ensure that his MEASAT sale would not be derailed in any way, Ananda decided to provide 1MDB with the bridge-financing package that would pave the way for the acquisition of the power assets. Ananda's private corporate vehicles provided guarantees on MYR 2 billion that made up the equity portion of the deal, which then allowed Malayan Banking and RHB, two state-controlled financial institutions, to pony up the roughly MYR 6 billion to complete the deal for the power-generation plants.

Low decided to leverage the newly acquired business to raise a new bond issue in order to pay down the equity portion Ananda's entities had helped raise, as well as the loans from Maybank and RHB. Low and 1MDB tapped Goldman Sachs to raise a USD 1.75 billion (MYR 5.39 billion) bond issue.

But with the Najib government reluctant to provide a fresh outright guarantee, Low had to turn to other sources. He could not tap his Saudi friends, who helped raise fictitious debts to siphon money from the first bond issue.

Low's high-rolling pals, led by Sheikh Mansour bin Zayed Al Nayan of the Abu Dhabi royal family, were eager to step into the breach because the Malaysian financier promised that there were huge amounts of money to be made by keeping the Najib slush fund humming. Sheikh Mansour, who was already making global headlines for his ownership of UK premier football club Manchester City, was also the chairman of the International Petroleum Investment Corp (IPIC), and Low sold the narrative to 1MDB and Najib that the Abu Dhabi state concern would guarantee a debt, removing any risk on the country's domestic financial system.

Again, Low impressed Ananda, who was keen to rid his company's books of any direct exposure to 1MDB. Ananda knew Tim Leissner, the Goldman Sachs head of Asia operations, sans Japan, and he wanted the banker to keep him constantly updated. All Goldman Sachs wanted was for a credible party to underwrite, or guarantee, the bond issue in order for the global bank to find customers who would in turn invest in the paper issues by 1MDB.

Sometime in mid-2012, Leissner, a wiry individual with closely cropped hair, flew to London to put the final touches to the new bond deal. Ananda would later recount to an occasional visitor to his office—on the 42nd floor of Maxis Tower, which was part of the Twin Tower complex in downtown KL—how Leissner would reveal the ease with which the deal was done. 'Low came down to pick him (Leissner) up at the lobby of the building wearing dark sweatpants and a loose shirt, and escorted him upstairs to meet Sheik Mansour. After half an hour, IPIC agreed to underwrite the bond,' Ananda said to me in one of our sessions. 'I know people in the Middle East, but this guy's

connections are impressive,' Ananda said of Low. But that admiration would quickly morph into scorn.

After the inflated acquisition was completed, Ananda's private entities and foundations that controlled his Tanjong business network made a donation of MYR 500 million to a charitable organization set up by 1MDB.

Was the charity donation a financial backhander for agreeing to an inflated price tag, or some form of carrot to do the MEASAT deal? We don't know, but Low had other plans and he was moving fast.

While doing all the back-channel talks to line up 1MDB's purchase of the Tanjong energy assets, Low was secretly in talks with Malaysia's only casino operator, the Genting Group. Genting also owned a power-generation plant, and its power sale concession agreement with the Malaysian electricity utility, Tenaga Nasional, was about to expire. As soon as the Tanjong deal was wrapped up, Goldman Sachs was instructed by 1MDB to raise another USD 1.75 billion bond issue that was again underwritten by Abu Dhabi's IPIC. 1MDB would pay roughly USD 775 million (MYR 2.39 billion) for Genting's two gas-fired power plants in Malaysia. Once again, the valuations were considered steep for power assets with concession agreements that were to expire in three years. And like Tanjong, the Genting units made a political contribution of USD 61 million to charities operated by Najib, establishing a pattern of how public funds were used to acquire private assets at premium prices in return for political backhanders.

The fundraising did not stop there. With IPIC displaying an insatiable craving to guarantee loans as a new source of business, Low and his Abu Dhabi buddies arranged

for Goldman Sachs to lead the fundraising of a separate ten-year USD 3 billion bond issue for 1MDB to finance its equity interest in a 50:50 joint venture with the Abu Dhabi government. All these deals received the personal backing of Najib and his government. By this point, 1MDB was saddled with debts of just under USD 12 billion (roughly MYR 40 billion) and the sovereign fund was soon making waves as the largest issuer of privately placed US-dollar debt in Asia.

Malaysia was also becoming one of the biggest clients for Goldman. Between 2011 and 2012, Goldman Sachs had stitched up bond issues for the state government of Sarawak and 1MDB amounting to USD 8.1 billion, in the process raking in fees of nearly USD 260 million. Leissner and his pal, Ng, had emerged as the masters of the Goldman universe in Asia. Low's ties with Ng grew as they plotted schemes to siphon money for both the Najib slush fund and for themselves.

Ananda, who had long fancied himself as Malaysia's most shrewd deal-maker, a 'financial engineer' as he once described himself to *The Asian Wall Street Journal,* was outmanoeuvred. While Low, Leissner, and Ng basked in their new-found fame and glory, Ananda was still stuck with his satellite assets. He later told the occasional visitor to his office that he had misjudged Low. 'He is going to be big trouble for Najib,' Ananda told to me during one of my interview sessions with him.

10

Turmoil at AmBank

Around 2010 and 2011, the Malaysian government's five-year electoral mandate was to conclude in barely two years and PM Najib was weighing his options. Najib could either call for snap polls, or sit out the full term and dissolve parliament after the first quarter of 2013. Whatever the timing, his party and coalition government would need large amounts of funding for the political campaign.

Within the Najib camp, all eyes turned to Low. He was barely twenty-nine and already impressing Najib by displaying the traits of a seasoned scheme artist. Apart from his unique ability to compartmentalize and juggle various financial manoeuvres, Low was soft-spoken, never mercurial even in the most tense of moments, and always understated in private encounters. His other side was his extravagant tastes, and a proclivity to throw lavish parties that drew the attention of the tabloids in New York.

Amid all of this, Low was locking the Najib government and the Malaysian people into the largest-ever debt

commitment entered into by any administration since independence in 1957. He held no position in any government agency. He had no official advisory role at 1MDB. While those outside Najib's circle, particularly Mahathir Mohamed's clique of cronies, began to view Low with a mix of envy and concern, there was nothing but admiration for Low as far as PM Najib was concerned. He may be 'rough around the edges', Najib remarked to one of his aides (the late Datuk Azlin Alias, who died in a helicopter crash in April 2015 that also claimed the life of senior UMNO man Jamaluddin Jarjis). Najib was suggesting that Low was sometimes reckless, but nevertheless his personal financial buccaneer.

Najib assigned all duties to Low when it came to bringing back the 1MDB-related funds that had been spirited away to offshore accounts. Low quickly began discussions with AmBank's Cheah and central bank governor Zeti on how to proceed. The first hurdle was coming up, requiring a narrative that would make the inflow of huge amounts of siphoned funds appear kosher. A grand subterfuge was necessary for Cheah to go along with the plan, and for Zeti to clear the regulatory path. Low suggested a plan by which AmBank would get notifications that Najib was expected to receive large funds from a senior member of the ruling family of Saudi Arabia. Letters from the highest levels of the Saudi government would be furnished to support the plan and this would get funds into Malaysia without encountering any regulatory obstacles.

The first letter, dated 1 February 2011, on the letterhead of the 'Private office of Saud Abdulaziz Al Saud' was titled 'Recognition of Contribution to The Islamic World' and it waxed lyrical about Najib. It read: 'I have been following your

work recently and I am impressed with the work that you have done to govern Malaysia using Islamic principles and how you are reintroducing Islam to the rest of the world in view of the current perception that many people have since 9/11 . . . In view of the friendship that we have developed over the years and your new ideas as a modern Islamic leader, I hereby grant you a sum of United States Dollars One Hundred Million (USD100,000,000) Only ('Gift') which shall be remitted to you at such times and in such manner as I deem fit. You shall have absolute discretion to determine how the Gift shall be utilised and I am confident that your actions will continue to promote Islam so it continues to flourish. This is merely a small gesture on my part but it is my way of contributing to the development of Islam to the world.'[2]

In a kingdom never short of princelings, there appears to be very little evidence of fact-checking by AmBank on the true identity of Prince Saud Abdulaziz. The letter should have also appeared incredulous to any seasoned banker. But that did not stop Cheah from leaning heavily on the dispatch to shoot off a note to Zeti on 9 February 2011, eight days on from the date of the letter. His note to Negara governor Zeti stated that, 'Further to our brief conversation, I would like to advise that the designated account . . . for the expected remittances would be "AmPrivate Banking – MR".'[3] It was by all accounts a stealth operation. The account was structured to

[2] Sadho Ram, 'Najib Shares "Documents" Claiming USD100 Million Came As 'Gift' From Saudi Arabian Royalty', SAYS, 11 September 2018, https://says.com/my/news/najib-shares-documents-claiming-usd100-million-came-as-gift-from-saudi-arabian-royalty.

[3] Quoted from the internal AmBank document that I reviewed.

ensure maximum confidentiality, even among senior members of the bank's top management, by attaching a unique internal coding and tagging. The prefix *Am* represented a loophole that puts the activities of the account outside AmBank's own compliance system, while 'MR' was the code reference for Mr Razak.

At this point, it is unclear how many people Cheah brought into the loop for Najib's account with AmBank. But Cheah knew that having Najib as a client would likely become an issue and Cheah's big conundrum was, at what point should he bring AmBank's foreign shareholder, Australian banking group ANZ, into the picture. He decided not to delay the matter and quickly reached out to his ANZ counterpart, Ashok Ramamurthy, who had previously been chief financial officer (CFO) at AmBank. Cheah informed ANZ's chief representative in Malaysia that Najib had decided to set up a personal account with the bank and that approval had been obtained from Negara. Ashok, a native of India who had migrated to New Zealand in 1988 before taking a senior position at ANZ, was taken aback by the disclosure. He asked Cheah why the PM had chosen AmBank and not a state-controlled financial institution, such as Maybank or CIMB, which was headed by Najib's younger brother, Nazir. Cheah responded that since the request came from the PM, he could not say 'no', and went on to add that Najib was expected to receive donations from overseas parties. Ashok, who had doubled as both CFO and deputy group managing director of AmBank, became uneasy but did not pursue the matter further with Cheah.

Along with his other ANZ colleagues, Ashok was more than curious about Cheah's access to the PM, which was

an invaluable connection when doing business in a country like Malaysia. Cheah, a pudgy man with a slow gait and easy smile, had studied economics at the University of Malaya and, before joining AmBank, had worked at a government agency set up specially to attract foreign direct investments into the country. Despite his long years at AmBank, Cheah was never a high-profile banker desiring media attention like many of his contemporaries. But after snaring the 1MDB deal, Cheah felt that a little self-promotion would not hurt. He never downplayed his access to Najib, which everyone at AmBank knew was through Low. He would often slip into private conversations with his heads of department that, among 'AmBank's board of directors, I have the best access to the prime minister'.

Between late February and November of 2011, AmPrivate Banking – MR received just under USD 100 million in four separate transactions from Saudi Arabia. Shortly after these deposits arrived in Najib's account, AmBank was furnished with another piece of correspondence on the same letterhead as before, dated 1 November 2011. The letter referred to the earlier note sent in February, and stated that, 'in addition to my earlier commitment, I hereby grant you an additional sum of up to United States Dollars Three Hundred and Seventy-Five Million (USD 375,000,000) Only (Gift), which shall be remitted to you at such time and in such manner as I deem fit either directly from my personal account or through my company bank accounts (such as Blackstone Asia Real Estate Partners Limited). You shall have absolute discretion to determine how the Gift should be utilised . . . I do not expect to receive any personal benefit whether directly or indirectly as a result of the Gift. The Gift should not in any

event be construed as an act of corruption since it is against the practice of Islam and I personally do not encourage such practices in any manner whatsoever.'[4]

Ashok took over as the group's CEO when Cheah retired from the position in the first quarter of 2012. Cheah, who remained AmBank's chief liaison to the Najib administration, was shunted upstairs in a glorified position as advisor to chairman Azman Hashim, one of the founders of the financial institution. Barely weeks after settling into his new position, Ashok was alerted by Bob Mofatt, another ANZ secondment who served as the chief of capital and balance sheet management at AmBank, that more than MYR 500 million (roughly USD 150 million) had been banked into the Najib account, and that the balance had been growing since December 2011. It was the first time that ANZ's chief representative in the Malaysian venture had discovered that the remittances were super-huge. Further, under global standards that deal with money laundering, the remittances clearly required the bank to raise what are typically referred to as suspicious transaction reports, or STRs, to their respective regulators.

Ashok, who had just turned fifty at the time, ordered an urgent internal review over the matter and a full disclosure of remittances received and the recipients of monies paid out by the account. When he questioned why this had been kept away from senior management, Ashok was told that the way the account 'AmPrivate Banking – MR' was set up with the prefix of '*Am*' represented a convenient loophole

[4] From a review of internal AmBank documents and interviews with executives from the financial institution.

in internal controls, and that it lay outside the purview of AmBank's compliance system on STRs, as it would have been seen as an entity within the bank itself.

Ashok, now nervous because of the clandestine workings around the Najib account, quickly initiated counter measures to protect himself and ANZ in a situation that increasingly had the makings of a potentially huge sandal.

If only he knew then how huge a scandal it was to become. In any case, Ashok quickly turned to AmBank's chairman Azman to help arrange for a personal meeting with Negara's Zeti to draw her attention to his most recent findings. The Negara governor's office finally reverted with a meeting in late September 2012. Ashok took Cheah along for the meeting at the governor's cavernous penthouse office within the central bank.

Zeti and Cheah have remained tight-lipped about the meeting. Based on conversations Ashok shared with several senior AmBank colleagues at the time, he delivered a note to Zeti that provided a brief timeline of Najib's account, detailing when the amounts were deposited and paid out. The letter noted that, from the time the account was opened in early 2011 and up until late July 2012, a total of USD 295 million (roughly MYR 907 million at the prevailing exchange rates) had been remitted in nine transactions. The senders of the funds were Prince Faisal bin Turkey Bandar Alsaud, the Ministry of Finance Riyadh, and Blackstone Asia Real Estate Partners, based in Singapore. During the same period, more than MYR 85.5 million had been paid out to various private companies, politically connected individuals, and elected representatives at both federal and state levels. Zeti took several minutes to review the letter and asked the AmBank

executives about Blackstone, which had been flagged as a company bank account in the second note of November 2011 from Prince Saud Abdulaziz to Najib. Ashok replied that his team had done some research, but their knowledge on the entity was limited.

What came after was more shocking. Zeti told both banking executives to refrain from using names when discussing the matter. She explained that she wanted to protect her office from listening devices but could not protect herself from lip-reading devices if they were being used. She then went on to say that she did not wish to retain a copy of the letter Ashok had prepared, lest it be seen by non-authorised parties. Zeti then advised Ashok to keep the letter safely and cautioned him to be careful when discussing the matter of Najib's account.

The monies kept flowing in and the growing subterfuge in the handling of Najib's account began to bother Ashok and the other ANZ secondees at AmBank more and more. Whether their concerns were brought to the attention of their bosses in Australia is not clear.

The prime minister's account was operating like a classic political slush fund that was receiving large amounts of funds from sources that AmBank knew very little about, and that the bank relied completely on representations and assurances made largely by Low, or people closely associated with him, over these funding sources. Some senior AmBank executives were also becoming a little apprehensive. But the concerns, if there were any, were placated by Negara's seemingly nonchalant stance towards Najib's account. That was good enough for the bank's founder, Azman, and his senior management.

But it was not good enough for Ashok, who wanted to keep his solid reputation with his bosses in ANZ intact, and was looking forward to returning to the group's headquarters, along Melbourne's Collins Street, on a promotion. In early April 2013, shortly after Najib announced the dissolution of parliament to make way for a general election the following May, more funds began pouring into AmPrivate Banking – MR, further spooking Ashok and his senior ANZ colleagues at AmBank.

With national polls just weeks away and growing speculation that the Najib-led National Front coalition faced the serious prospect of defeat, Ashok decided to update Zeti on the status of the PM's account. He wrote that, since his last discussion in September with the Negara governor over the account named AmPrivate Banking – MR, more than USD 755.99 million (roughly MYR 2.31 billion) had been remitted into the account in six separate transactions, from three separate sources. Riyadh's Prince Faisal bin Turkey bin Bandar Alsaud remitted a total of USD 24.9 million, while Singapore-based Blackstone remitted USD 49.9 million. The single largest chunk, USD 681 million, came from a little-known BVI entity known as Tanore Finance Corp.

In summary, since the account was created in 2011, AmPrivate Banking – MR had received deposits amounting to MYR 3.22 billion and paid out MYR 372 million. The interest earned by the account amounted to MYR 13.6 million.

After dispatching the letter, Ashok went further. He asked for a meeting with Negara deputy governor Nor Shamsiah Mohd Yunus, who would later speak to him over the telephone. Ashok later confided in his Malaysian ANZ colleagues that Shamsiah was also not comfortable with the significant amounts of funds that were being deposited and

paid out. But he also noted to Zeti's No. 2 that AmBank's checks on the anti-money laundering (AML) and countering the financing of terrorism (CFT) checking mechanisms had raised no red flags.

In a country like Malaysia, where remittances in excess of MYR 10,000 by 'ordinary citizens' can trigger official scrutiny, why Negara chose to accept verbal assurances from AmBank without further investigating the activities at the AmPrivate Banking – MR account remains as one of the central bank's biggest lapses in the 1MDB affair.

A pattern was emerging at Negara. When it came to 1MDB, the central bank governor, Zeti Akhtar Aziz, played the role of the eyes-wide-shut regulator.

11

Election 2013

It was his election year and Najib stepped into 2013 a very confident man. His rise to the Prime Minister's Office was not smooth, but way from bumpy. After the death of his father—Malaysia's second prime minister, Abdul Razak Hussein—in early 1976, Najib's mother, Rahah Mohamed Noah, was persuaded by the country's aristocratic elite that her son should embrace politics. Najib took the plunge at twenty-three, a somewhat tender age for politics, and quickly began making records. He became the youngest person in Malaysia to be elected to parliament, the youngest person to be appointed a federal deputy minister and, subsequently, the youngest politician to become chief minister of his home state of Pahang, in the central region of peninsular Malaysia.

When he stepped into the prime ministership in 2009 to replace Badawi—forced into retirement by Mahathir, who hounded him while he was in office—Najib became the first descendent of a former prime minister to take on the country's top job.

The only thing missing in Najib's impressive political CV was a public mandate that he could call his own. The end of the government's five-year term was fast approaching and Najib needed to pick a date to dissolve parliament and call for fresh elections.

By most accounts he was confident of a major victory, to reverse the stunning losses that the ruling coalition had suffered in the 2008 general election. His sleek PR juggernaut of local and foreign consultants, financed largely by 1MDB-related funds, was telling him that a 5 per cent swing in voter sentiment away from the opposition would deliver a huge win for his National Front.

Najib and his wife, Rosmah, also had a superstitious streak and were known to consult shamans, soothsayers, fortune tellers, local ethnic Malay practitioners of the 'dark arts' known as *bomohs*, and masters of feng shui (an arm of geomancy said to marshal a cosmic energy known as *qi*). Husband and wife aimed to look into current events to see what they may portend for the future, and to seek guidance on how to sidestep any potential misfortune that lay ahead. After being sufficiently satisfied that their mystic intermediaries had interrogated their respective gods for guidance, Najib decided to seek his public mandate—Malaysia's 13th general election since independence from Britain in 1957—on 5 May 2013. Najib was told that anything negative in the association of the number 13, to both the position of the poll in Malaysia's history and the year he was calling Malaysians to test his popularity, had been neutralized by their collective spiritual intercession.

While Najib's UMNO fared well in the general election, he nevertheless received a rude surprise and the GE13

result delivered a political body blow. UMNO, the linchpin in Najib's coalition, increased the number of seats it held in the 222-member parliament to 88, from 79 in the 2008 poll, largely due to strong support from ethnic Malays in rural areas. But its non-Malay political partners were decimated, rejected wholesale by Malaysian voters in urban areas. So, as UMNO improved its parliamentary clout, the National Front's share of parliamentary seats fell to 133, from the 140 secured in 2009. The coalition also lost the popular vote for the first time in Malaysia's history, but retained control of government because of the decades-old programme of electoral gerrymandering.

Suddenly, the UMNO-led National Front, one of the longest-existing ruling coalitions in the world, was staring at an existential crisis. Najib was starting to feel the heat as factions began to take shape in UMNO ahead of the party's internal elections later in the year.

His world began to look dark. Then it got a little darker, when the first major news exposé on 1MDB was published in mid-June 2013.

The story appeared in an experimental start-up digital magazine that I led, in collaboration with a Malaysian news group called The Edge Communications. *The Edge Review* was a digital weekly covering business and politics in Southeast Asia. It began publication in late March 2013 and produced its last despatch in June 2015. I parted ways with the rights to the start-up and ownership of the content that had been produced. During its more than two years of delivering original Southeast Asian content, *The Edge Review* won several regional media awards for its high-end journalism. The cover story in the 19 July 2013 issue was headlined

1MDB: Malaysia's US$12 billion hot potato. The report was based on official corporate documents filed at government agencies and deep background interviews with bankers, government officials, and executives at the state-owned fund. It provided the first serious peek into the affairs at 1MDB and won the prestigious award for Excellence in Business Reporting from the Society of Publishers in Asia (SOPA). The story headlined **The Big Gamble**[5] was singled out by the SOPA judges for putting the '1MDB story into context and conveying the potential for trouble'.

The piece, published in *The Edge Review* on 25 July 2013, is reproduced at the end of this chapter.

The exposé stirred a hornet's nest in the Najib camp. The PM was upset.

The story cut very close to the bone, Low himself told me over a telephone conversation an hour after the story came online. 'He is worried that his political opponents in UMNO will turn 1MDB into an issue at the party election in November,' said Low, who was also a little concerned that he himself could come under attack.

At that particular juncture, those concerns were misplaced. Apart from the slight roiling of waters in the Najib clique, the story did not trigger much reaction. I wondered why the report did not lead to a surge in follow-up reporting by foreign news organizations. To use contemporary news production parlance, it had all the elements of a 'sexy' saga: a seriously scandalized prime minister, who also had the cloud

---

[5] https://2014.sopawards.com/wp-content/uploads/2014/05/The-Big-Gamble.pdf

of murder allegations over him; a ruling coalition with a long record of extractive policies that resulted in billions of dollars in taxpayer monies being channelled to vested interests; and an international banking giant, Goldman Sachs, that was clearly facilitator to the looting. It was easier to understand the lukewarm response at home.

Najib remained politically powerful despite the electoral setback, and it was also in the interest of the political elite to keep a lid on the 1MDB affair because so many people and agencies were complicit.

All of this changed quickly after the UMNO party elections in November 2013. The party congress brought into the open simmering tensions between Najib and his No. 2, Muhyiddin Yassin, who was UMNO's deputy president as well as deputy prime minister. There were no contests for the top two positions in the party, a traditional practice ostensibly intended to project unity. But the bruising battles for the three vice president positions and the twenty-five slots in the party's powerful policy-making Supreme Council turned into a public spectacle—in all its hues of black, white, and grey—that sent one message: UMNO was lurching into another crisis.

Najib's take-no-prisoners approach, a strategy that was lumped on him by his political advisors after the National Front's poor showing in the May general election, worked too well. Najib's money-flushed political juggernaut, greased generously by Low's diversion of 1MDB funds, helped him dominate UMNO. The three vice president slots were comfortably snatched by UMNO leaders aligned with Najib, together with positions in the powerful Supreme Council.

The results of the party elections successfully marginalized Muhyiddin, and sent a clear signal that he was no longer in favour. Another casualty was Mukhriz Mahathir, the youngest son of former PM Mahathir. Najib's dispatching of Mukhriz was intended to make clear to Mahathir that UMNO was now his party.

The political schemers and operatives in Najib's inner circle were chuffed with the outcome of the party elections. Their boss had emerged victorious. While the ageing Mahathir remained a potential thorn, the former PM was manageable. Najib was in full control and the only real worry was opposition leader Anwar Ibrahim.

Najib's political spooks, both in his inner circles and the dark ops agencies in the police and the military, worked overtime. They constantly fed him intelligence reports that Anwar was scheming to woo disgruntled politicians in the National Front to defect and bring down an already fragile government, along with the Front, which had long held popular support in consecutive general elections, albeit with the machinations of electoral gerrymandering.

But Muhyiddin was more than a fleeting worry. His historically close ties to Anwar made him a potential threat, because he could lead the disgruntled among those in the government to back Anwar. But Najib was convinced by his inner circle that Muhyiddin had to be politically neutered, and keeping the enemy close, as his deputy in UMNO and deputy PM in government, would be the best chess move.

The two men were like chalk and cheese. While Najib's rise to power had a lot to do with his strong political pedigree—largely sourced from his father, Malaysia's second PM—and his own affable demeanour that won him a

following, Muhyiddin was a different animal. Aloof, dour, and standoffish, Muhyiddin never bothered about building a strong grassroots appeal. He generally spoke down to his constituents. A politically shrewd fox from the southern Johor state that neighbours Singapore, he steadily climbed up the political ladder with scheming and treachery. Najib's deputy was the ultimate usurper, a chameleon-like political operative with a long history of backstabbing.

Muhyiddin went into government service after graduating from the University of Malaya in 1971 with honours in economics and Malay studies, a stepping stone for anyone with designs on a career in domestic politics. An ambitious self-promoter, Muhyiddin quickly caught the eye of the Johor chief minister of the time, Othman Saat, a fast-emerging, power-gathering warlord. Othman grafted Muhyiddin as a senior political aide and brought him into the UMNO fold by making him a member in his own ward, Pagoh, in the mid-1970s. In the national election of 1978, Muhyiddin contested in the Pagoh parliamentary constituency and won easily.

Four years later, he was appointed as a deputy minister in the new Mahathir government that had come to power a year earlier, in mid-July 1981. Muhyiddin's appointment was a chess move by Deputy Prime Minister Musa Hitam, another Johor politician who wanted to oust Chief Minister Othman.

Muhyiddin embraced his role as a pawn in a bigger political play, switched allegiances, and defeated Othman to become chief of the Pagoh UMNO division in May 1984. When Musa resigned as deputy PM in February 1986, citing irreconcilable differences with Mahathir, Muhyiddin switched

camp again, and aligned himself with the ascendant Anwar. In August of the same year, Muhyiddin contested in the state and parliamentary elections, won both convincingly and was sworn in as the chief minister of Johor, leapfrogging over many more senior and hugely popular candidates, who littered the wayside because of their association with Musa.

Muhyiddin presided over a booming Johor economy, openly used his influence and position to support his business cronies, and became one of Malaysia's wealthiest politicians. Muhyiddin's ability to dispense patronage, and his ties to Anwar, quickly turned him into a strong candidate for future national leadership.

But Muhyiddin's avarice would catch up with him. A privately owned company called Stamford Holdings sued Muhyiddin and his close business acolyte, Syed Mokhtar Albukhary—who would later become the most favoured corporate son of the Mahathir government—for recovery and damages amounting to nearly MYR 1 billion (roughly USD 250 million at the prevailing exchange rate). Muhyiddin had used his power as chief minister to forcibly acquire a 2,640-hectare property at a huge discount off the market value. The widely publicized dispute was eventually settled out of court, but the case left a nasty stain on the UMNO-led government, which at the time was wracked by a series of financial scandals. In what was widely seen as a reprimand, Mahathir forced Muhyiddin to give up the Johor chief ministership and yanked him back to the federal government to head the Ministry of Youth and Sports in May 1995. The reassignment to a very junior ministry hurt his political prestige. Muhyiddin remained as a minister in the Mahathir cabinet but his rise in UMNO had been undercut.

Serving time in political purgatory would pay dividends for Muhyiddin. When Malaysia's political tumult hit in mid-1998, Anwar fell out with his boss, Mahathir, over differences on how to handle a raging regional financial crisis that had devastated Thailand and later deposed Indonesian strongman Suharto. Through this time, Muhyiddin was out of the firing line, and he quickly cosied up behind Mahathir's new deputy, Abdullah Ahmad Badawi. Muhyiddin had lobbied hard to become Abdullah's deputy when Mahathir retired in November 2003. But Abdullah was pressured by Mahathir to pick Najib. Frustrated over being side-lined, Muhyiddin led the charge after Abdullah's UMNO fared badly in the 2008 general election, which resulted in Najib becoming prime minister in 2009.

Muhyiddin bided his time as Najib's loyal deputy in UMNO and the government, hoping to seize the day on any of Najib's missteps. But that opportunity never came. Even after Najib's government performed worse than in the previous election, there was no way he could mount any subversive campaign. As stated previously, Najib took complete control of UMNO in the party's polls in late 2013. Muhyiddin had no allies in UMNO. Isolated politically, Muhyiddin realized that he could not stage a coup against Najib in UMNO. He needed to latch onto something bigger, something that would force Najib to hand over the nation's highest office to him.

Thousands of miles away, a heavily tattooed, rogue Swiss IT executive was emerging, and he would become crucial to Muhyiddin's plans.

COVER STORY

1MDB

The Big Gamble

Secretive Malaysian fund stirs controversy at home and abroad

By Leslie Lopez / Kuala Lumpur

Sometime in September 2009, currency traders at Malaysia's central bank, Bank Negara, were jolted by huge purchases of US dollars in the domestic currency market and quickly decided to halt the selling pressure on the local currency. They were promptly told to stand down by their superiors.

The buildup of US dollar positions on that day paved the way for state-owned 1 Malaysia Development Bhd. (1MDB) to move US$1 billion out of the country for an investment in a British Virgin Islands entity.

"At the time, no one knew where the money was headed or why such a large amount was being taken out," said one senior Kuala Lumpur-based currency trader familiar with the episode.

"It was a company we needed to watch, because it came out of nowhere and showed clout," said another chief dealer at a foreign bank in Kuala Lumpur.

These days, 1MDB isn't just raising eyebrows. The secretive investment arm of the government is sending shockwaves through international bond markets and raising concern at home with its aggressive borrowings, opaque financial manoeuvres and risky bets. It is also becoming a hot political potato for Prime Minister Najib Abdul Razak's administration.

Opposition politicians insist that 1MDB is part strategic investment arm and part political slush fund for the Najib government, because of its generous financial handouts to key constituencies of the ruling Barisan Nasional (National Front) coalition.

In just over four years, 1MDB has racked up borrowings of more than US$11.97 billion (RM38 billion), corporate documents and published accounts reviewed by The Edge Review show. This huge accumulation of debt is against a backdrop of paltry profits, derived largely from the shuffling of assets on its Cayman Island investment and the revaluation of properties purchased at steep discounts from the government.

No Southeast Asian entity has accumulated so much debt in such a short time, and because the borrowings carry the implicit guarantee of the Malaysian government, bankers and economists say that 1MDB is emerging as a serious contingent liability for the Najib administration.

"1MDB doesn't have strong cash flows and, at the rate it is borrowing, sooner or later the government will have to step in to take responsibility," says a chief executive of a Malaysian bank, echoing a widely held view of 1MDB among the Kuala Lumpur business community.

For now, a government bailout may not appear imminent. But close scrutiny of 1MDB's affairs reveal potential trouble spots that bankers and investment analysts say could suddenly spin out of control and plunge Malaysia into an explosive business scandal.

One potential flashpoint is 1MDB's original US$1 billion investment in 2009 in 1MDB PetroSaudi Ltd, an entity domiciled in the British Virgin Islands. 1MDB's most recent accounts lodged with Malaysia's Registrar of Companies show that the original investment has since more than doubled in value to US$2.3 billion, and is now "reinvested" in a company registered in the Cayman Islands. But bankers say that spectacular profits, derived from a series of financial flips with little- known entities, have raised concerns about the security of the venture.

1MDB's dizzying buildup of debt is also drawing international attention because of the fund's cosy relations with international banking powerhouse Goldman Sachs, which critics say has allowed the US firm to charge supernormal fees.

Over the last two years, Goldman has single-handedly structured and underwritten US$6.5 billion in bonds for 1MDB. Taken together with the US$1.6 billion the US firm raised for the state government of Sarawak on Borneo, Goldman ranks as the largest underwriter of bonds in Malaysia, outranking local powerhouses such as Malayan Banking and CIMB Group, which have long cornered the debt-raising business of state-owned entities.

1MDB declined to comment officially for this article but several government officials and financial executives involved in 1MDB's investments spoke to The Edge Review on condition of anonymity and argued that the picture isn't as tenuous as it appears.

Repayments on a portion of its loans in coming months will cut 1MDB's debts to roughly RM34 billion, which is backed by assets valued at roughly RM38 billion, they say. These include liquid assets of cash and other securities valued at RM16 billion.

The officials insist that the Cayman Islands investment is safe and a planned listing of the group's power- generation assets, set for sometime in the first half of next year, is expected to raise close to RM5 billion and strengthen its financial position.

"Viewed in a snapshot, there are some issues (that could be of concern). But the story going forward is positive," says one senior government official, who acknowledges that the veil of secrecy surrounding 1MDB has fuelled controversy over the fund's activities.

Private economists and bankers, however, aren't so sanguine. They note that 1MDB's huge borrowings are cause for concern for the Malaysian economy because of rising public sector debt.

Malaysia has consistently run budget deficits since the currency crisis that struck the region in mid- 1997. That, in turn, has raised the nation's accumulated public debt, which currently stands at 53 per cent of the country's gross domestic product – the highest among the 10-member Association of South East Asian Nations (Asean).

The ratio of debt-to-GDP is a broad measure of the health of an economy and Malaysia has a self-imposed ceiling of 55 per cent. The problem, say private economists, is that the ratio doesn't take into account liabilities of state-linked enterprises such as 1MDB, which have been on a borrowing binge to fund development activities.

The following account of 1MDB's rise from a secretive state-owned strategic investment fund to one of Malaysia's

most debt-laden entities is based on documents reviewed by The Exige Review and interviews with dozens of bankers, financial consultants and government officials over the last four years.

Seeds of 1MDB were sown in early 2009, when businessman Low Tack Jho, who enjoys close relations with Prime Minister Najib, mooted the idea of creating a fund to manage the resources of the northeastern Terengganu state in Peninsular Malaysia.

Terengganu is a key oil-and-gas-producing state, but it has a high incidence of poverty because of poor management of its wealth over the last four decades. The plan called for the setting up of a 10-billion ringgit fund, called the Terengganu Investment Authority, with capital raised equally by the state and federal governments through a bond issue.

The Terengganu government got cold feet, however, when it realised that the annual repayments for the bonds would prove too much for the state's coffers. But Najib liked the idea of a strategic investment fund, and, shortly after assuming the premiership in April 2009, signed off on a government guarantee for the new fund to issue Islamic bonds to raise RM5 billion of seed capital. The money was quickly raised and the Terengganu Investment Authority was renamed Malaysia Development Bhd.

Almost immediately, the fund attracted controversy. Bankers attacked the maiden 30-year bond issue, because the coupon, which is the periodic interest payment a bond investor receives, was priced at an annual rate of 5.75 per cent, a level considered high for a government guaranteed bond. While there are no perfect comparisons, bonds issued by Malaysia's state oil corporation Petronas carry an annual coupon rate of around 3.6 per cent.

1MDB didn't waste any time spending the money it raised. Barely four months after the bond issue, the fund invested US$1 billion (roughly RM3.4 billion at the time) to acquire a 40 per cent interest in a joint-venture concern with PetroSaudi International Ltd., a little-known concern incorporated in Saudi Arabia.

The fund's move to plough 70 per cent of its seed capital into a single venture was seen as reckless. By mid-2010, 1MDB was turning to Malaysian and foreign banks for more funding, triggering speculation that the fund's aggressive bets had gone sour and would need fresh capital injections from the government.

At the time, 1MDB executives dismissed talk of financial trouble and insisted that the fund had turned a profit in its first year of operation. Audited accounts lodged with Malaysia's Registrar of Companies show that the fund applied some fancy financial footwork to register a profit for the fiscal year ended March 2010. According to the accounts, 1MDB sold back its investment in the venture it controlled with PetroSaudi for a profit of roughly RM630 million barely six months after making the original investment. That deal helped 1MDB show a first year profit of RM424.6 million.

While the headline number appeared impressive, the nature of the deal only stoked more questions, because it was a cashless transaction. After investing RM3.4 billion in cash for the venture, the state-owned fund accepted an 11-year repayment scheme structured like an Islamic bond, which included commitments from a private concern incorporated in tax havens such as the British Virgin Islands.

The deal was also red-flagged in 1MDB's account for the year ended March 2010 by its external auditors KPMG, which suggested that the transaction was of potential concern. In its

report to shareholders of the company, KPMG flagged the transaction under the heading

"Emphasis of Matter." It noted that the valuation of the transaction was undertaken by a third party and that 1MDB's management "believes that PSI (PetroSaudi International) is in good standing" and has the ability to meet all obligations. (An "Emphasis of Matter" is an item that is typically included in an independent auditor's report to highlight fundamental uncertainties that could have an adverse impact on a company in the future.)

1MDB's latest published accounts show that it disposed of its PetroSaudi investment in September last year to an undisclosed external party for US$2.318 billion. But bankers and analysts question why the state-owned fund has yet to bring the money back to help finance its other ventures.

Government officials and financial executives involved in 1MDB say that these concerns are misplaced and the funds will be used to take advantage of new overseas investment opportunities.

"Bringing the money back would also result in some hefty forex (foreign exchange) loses," argues one government official. The original investment was made when the Malaysian currency stood at just under RM3.4 to the US dollar. It is now at RM3.187 to the greenback.

While questions around the PetroSaudi venture aren't likely to go away anytime soon, attention is now focused on 1MDB's build-up of debt through the issuance of bonds in the international markets in order to invest in the property and electricity-generation sectors.

Over the last 18 months, 1MDB has raised close to US$9.37 billion (RM29.8 billion) in new debt. A big chunk of the debt – US$5.47 billion (RM17.4 billion) – was raised to acquire power

generation assets in Malaysia and plants in Bangladesh, Egypt and the United Arab Emirates. The fund also raised another US$3 billion in late April to finance its equity interest in a 50:50 joint venture with the Abu Dhabi government.

The bond issues, which together represent one of the biggest privately placed issuance of US dollar debt in Asia in recent years, were structured singlehandedly by Goldman Sachs, and rival bankers argue that 1MDB and the Malaysian government overpaid for the deal.

Just like 1MDB's first bond issue of RM5 billion, the coupon rate attached to the bonds that Goldman structured was well above prices for the debt of state-owned entities. "Bonds typically carry a premium of between 10 to 20 basis points over the sovereign debt. The close to 300 basis point is really pricey," says one international bond trader.

Bankers say that 1MDB's decision to use only Goldman, which reportedly has earned more than US$250 million in fees from its Malaysian government-related advisory and bond issues, came at a cost to the Malaysian taxpayer.

"It would have been less expensive in terms of how the bonds were priced and also on fees if the deal were done by a consortium (of banks)," says a chief executive of a Malaysian bank.

But government officials say 1MDB can't be compared to other state-owned entities, such as national oil corporation Petronas and state-controlled power utility Tenaga Nasional, which regularly tap the international financial markets for funding.

They note that 1MDB only received RM1 million in equity funding from the government when it was incorporated and the government has been reluctant to provide guarantees for its bonds.

"Without any assets to show, turning to a rating agency is risky," says one financial executive who is involved in the fund's financial affairs. He adds that the fund's financial standing in international markets is improving and the build-up of assets has helped 1MDB cut the pricing of its bonds. For example, the most recent US$3 billion placement by Goldman carried a coupon of 4.4 per cent, compared to 5.9 per cent for its first bond issue.

Government officials and financial executives close to 1MDB also insist that Goldman's involvement was above board. They point out that Goldman secured the first mandate in June 2012 for a jumbo US$1.75 billion deal on the insistence of the International Petroleum Investment Company (IPIC), an investment company of the Abu Dhabi government, which was guaranteeing the bond issue. As for the mandate for the US$3 billion bond in late April, Goldman had to compete with other international players such as Standard Chartered and Morgan Stanley.

Critics of 1MDB's diversification into the energy sector say that the fund paid a hefty premium for Tanjong Energy, a portfolio of regional energy assets owned by tycoon T. Ananda Krishnan, and Genting Sanyen Power, the 17-ycar-old power plant controlled by Malaysian gaming and leisure group Genting Bhd., which is publically listed.

1MDB paid US$2.67 billion (RM8.5 billion) for Tanjong Energy and US$723 million for Genting Sanyen. The long-term concessions held by Tanjong and Genting were close to expiry at the time of the purchase, and energy industry executives say that the value of the aging facilities was roughly 50 per cent of what was paid.

"Even if these companies had secured fresh extensions to the power sale agreements, the values would still be at a discount of what was paid," says a chief executive of a

boutique financial consultancy that specialises in the regional power sector.

Opposition politicians have also attacked the purchases, arguing that the hefty premiums 1MDB paid were designed to allow private companies to channel political contributions back to the ruling National Front coalition headed by Najib. Politicians and bankers close to the NF say that Tanjong and companies linked to Ananda contributed more than RM400 million to charity foundations linked to 1MDB, while Genting declared contributions of over RM190 million to charitable organisations linked to the state-owned fund for the first quarter of this year.

Government officials interviewed refused to disclose donations 1MDB-linked foundations have received from the private sector, saying only that such contributions were not linked to the state-owned fund's corporate transactions.

The official also defended the pricing of the power assets by 1MDB, arguing that the move was part of a larger government strategy to wrest control of power generation assets, which were privatised during the 1990s under former premier Mahathir Mohamad's government.

"On a stand alone basis, the acquisitions appear on the high side. But when taken as a collective asset, we believe that the purchase price can be defended," says one government official involved in the reorganisation of 1MDB assets.

The Tanjong and Genting power plants have a combined generation capacity of 4,700 megawatts, and 1MDB hopes to increase it up to 6,100 megawatts with its planned acquisition of another Malaysian private power concern, Jimah Power, for RM1.2 billion (US$377 million). The power plants will be merged into a new entity in coming months and 1MDB plans to make a public offering for the new company to raise as much as RM5 billion sometime in the first half of next year.

Apart from the power sector, government officials involved in 1MDB argue that the property sector will help shore up the group's finances. The fund owns 550 acres of prime land around Kuala Lumpur, which it intends to develop over 15 years.

"Energy and property will be the game changers going forward," says one government official seconded to 1MDB.

GOLDMAN SACHS' BOND UNDERWRITING IN MALAYSIA

	US$ BILLION
Sarawak government in 2011 and 2012	1.6
1MDB	
– Tanjong Energy	1.75
– Genting Sanyen	1.75
– 10-year bond	3.0
Total	8.1

Source: The Edge Review Research

1 MDB FINANCIAL SNAPSHOT (FOR THE YEAR-ENDED MARCH)

	2010	2011	2012
Total Assets (RM billion)	4.955	8.143	9.534
Total Borrowings (RM billion)	4.390	6.689	7.815
Profit (RM million)	426.607	544.343	44.733

Source: Annual Reports filed at the Registrar of Companies | (US$1 = RM 3.19)

PetroSaudi International Ltd

- PetroSaudi International, a privately owned oil exploration and production company, was founded in 2005 by Tarek Essam Ahmad Obaid.
- With offices in Saudi Arabia, England and Switzerland, PetroSaudi has ventured into oil and gas developments in the Caspian Sea and oil fields that straddle the border of Turkmenistan and oil-rich Azerbaijan.
- It formed a joint-venture with 1MDB in September 2009 through a company called 1MDB PetroSaudi Ltd, incorporated in the British Virgin Islands, with 1MDB holding 40 per cent and PetroSaudi the remainder.
- 1MDB pumped in US$1 billion (RM3.49 billion at the time) into the joint-venture concern and in end-March 2010 sold its interest for US$1.2 billion (RM4.14 billion at the time) financed by a 11-year repayment scheme through an Islamic financial structure that carried as interest rate of 8.67 per cent annually. In a nutshell, 1MDB would earn roughly RM359 million annually and receive the full sum for the divestment 11 years later.
- 1MDB invests an additional RM1.57 billion under a similar Islamic financial structure, which carried an interest charge of 8.25 per cent annually and a bullet repayment in five years.
- In September 2012 1MDB exits from complex financial structure with PetroSaudi and walks away with proceeds of US$2.32 billion.
- Tarek Obaid's other investment in Malaysia is a controlling stake in UBG Bhd., an investment holding company previously controlled by the family of Taib Mahmud, the chief minister of the Sarawak state on Borneo. UBG, which is no longer listed on the Malaysian stock exchange,

is held by Obaid through his wholly owned subsidiary PetroSaudi International Seychelles. He acquired the company in early 2010.

Research by The Edge Review

12

The Blackmailer, Blogger, and Crony Businessman

Things were not working out for Xavier Andre Justo, a Swiss national of Spanish descent, at PetroSaudi International. After a year as head of the IT division and administrator of a couple of subsidiaries, his bosses Tarek Obaid and Patrick Mahoney decided to terminate his employment. Justo was raking up huge bills with his expense account at fancy restaurants in London's Knightsbridge and Covent Garden. Obaid had known Justo for many years and tolerated his friend's behaviour. But Mahoney was less forgiving and eventually convinced his partner that Justo had to be let go.

Sometime in mid-March 2012, Justo got wind that he was about to be let off. He had just married his partner, Laura, and began to worry about his financial security. The settlement package would not last long, and Justo needed something that he could later exploit for cash. The huge sums of funds that had been injected into the company two years earlier, from a concern known as 1Malaysia Development Berhad, were flowing into very opaque schemes designed

by Justo's bosses. As head of the IT division at PetroSaudi, Justo supervised the email traffic with regards to the 1MDB funds, but he understood little about them. All he knew was, something dodgy was going on.

Weeks before he left in late April, Justo had managed to download more than 90 gigabytes of data, including emails, documents, and other material.

Sometime in mid-2013, the bosses at PetroSaudi in London began receiving threats from their troublesome former IT executive, who by this time had settled down in Thailand's resort island of Phuket with his wife and newborn son. The message was clear: PetroSaudi would either pay CHF 3.5 million (Swiss Francs, which at that point converted to about USD 3.85 million), or risk public disclosure of a trove of sensitive emails that he had secretly appropriated through bulk downloads while he remained in employment. PetroSaudi rebuffed his demands and, in October of that year, Mahoney decided to personally engage with Justo to get him off their backs. A meeting was arranged in the lavish Shangri-La Hotel, on the banks of the Chao Phraya in Bangkok, where Mahoney told Justo that not a single cent would be paid to the former employee. If he persisted with the blackmail, PetroSaudi would file a criminal complaint over his theft of company data.

Justo backed off, but subsequently tapped his network of friends as he schemed to sell the stolen information. In January the following year, Justo made contact with an old banking acquaintance, Christian Frampton, and discussed the material that he had appropriated, involving his previous employers and 1MDB, which was by then starting to make news both in Malaysia and internationally. Frampton told

Justo that he knew a London-based businessman, Kamal Siddiqi, who was known to have strong ties with Malaysia, as well as being a close friend of former PM Mahathir Mohamad. Siddiqi, hailing from India and now a British citizen, was the controlling shareholder of Fraser-Nash and enjoyed unparalleled access to the Mahathir administration. He was a regular dinner guest at Mahathir's house when he visited Malaysia. Siddiqi was also a beneficiary of financial grants from the Malaysian government for research into electric cars, a subject of long-standing fascination for the Malaysian leader.

Nothing ever came out of the scheme that Siddiqi had convinced the Malaysian government to finance. But that did not dull Mahathir's close friendship with the entrepreneur, who was in turn always grateful. Siddiqi passed on Frampton's information to Mahathir, who was intrigued but wanted it to play out publicly before deciding whether to weigh in.

Siddiqi's next port of call was a British blogger, who had carved for herself a reputation for exposing government corruption and environmental destruction in the Malaysian state of Sarawak on Borneo Island, where she was born. An aggressive self-promoter, Clare Rewcastle Brown, who once worked as a journalist in the BBC World Service, was given to exaggeration after she decided to move onto social media platforms. She embraced sensationalism, the 'shoot first and ask questions second' approach, a brand of reporting that won her both admirers and detractors. There were other clouds. Her brother-in-law, the former British PM Gordon Brown—once described as a person who could brighten up a room simply by leaving it—gave her both celebrity status and notoriety, because her husband, Andrew Brown,

had been caught up in an embarrassing expenses scandal at 10 Downing Street in 2009.

By the time Siddiqi approached Brown, her Sarawak campaign was on its last legs and she needed to latch onto something new. She quickly seized on what Frampton was offering via Siddiqi. By all indications, it is more than likely Frampton was never in contact with Brown. Siddiqi gave Brown Justo's mobile co-ordinates in Thailand and Brown made contact sometime in mid-2014, making travel plans to see the former PetroSaudi executive and peddler of stolen data. The two first met at The Athenee Hotel in downtown Bangkok, where both Justo and Brown exchanged credentials—he showed proof of his employment in PetroSaudi and she established herself as a journalist-cum-blogger with strong contacts in Malaysia. There were two other meetings at the same Bangkok venue, in August and October that year, where Justo showed Brown more emails and documents related to PetroSaudi. Brown took particular interest in an email attachment with details of a joint venture between PetroSaudi and 1MDB, Justo would later recall. Brown believed the material Justo was peddling was authentic and, if she could get access to all of it, she was certain she had a blockbuster story. All she had to do was raise the USD 3 million Justo was insisting on.

Brown zeroed in on the Anwar Ibrahim camp. It was the most obvious target. Malaysian politics was starting to overheat again, with rumours about possible defections by elected members of parliament from Najib Abdul Razak's weakened coalition government. The defectors might want to throw in their lot with the Anwar-led opposition alliance. To get Anwar out of the way, Najib turned to the black-ops

playbook of former prime minister, Mahathir. Using Malaysia's then-pliant judiciary, the Najib government got the Court of Appeals, the country's second-highest judicial panel, to hear a second sexual complaint involving Anwar that alleged sodomy, which had been earlier thrown out by Malaysia's High Court. (In 1998, Anwar had been charged and found guilty of corruption and sodomy, and sentenced to jail.) As expected, the Court of Appeal overturned the 2012 High Court verdict and found Anwar guilty in March 2014. Anwar was allowed to appeal against the conviction at the Federal Court, the apex decision-making body in the judiciary. Anwar's appeal was set for some time in early 2015.

Brown approached Anwar's daughter, Nurul Izzah Anwar, a senior politician herself, about the material Justo was peddling. Nurul told Brown that the opposition would be interested in 1MDB, which it suspected was being used as a political slush fund by Najib. Anwar's daughter further suggested that payment to Justo could be in the form of contract awards in the future, when the opposition wrested control of government. Justo rejected the deal. He wanted his money there and then. An undeterred Brown continued to hawk Justo's wares to whoever would listen.

About the same time, Muhyiddin Yassin, Najib's deputy both in UMNO and government, began to sense that his boss was becoming politically vulnerable, particularly over the controversial 1MDB affair and the questions surrounding it. The pressure on Najib was growing. It was a constant fight to put out political bushfires lit by Anwar, who was staring at the prospect of returning to jail if he lost his appeal in the Federal Court. While prime minister and opposition leader sparred, Muhyiddin, who had no base in UMNO, began reaching

out to other forces in the country's powerful civil service, security agencies, and business elite as part of a broader plan to undermine Najib. One of the people Muhyiddin became close to was a pugnacious Malaysian businessman, himself desperately seeking a new political patron.

Tong Kooi Ong rose on Malaysia's corporate ladder in the first half of the 1990s by riding on the coat-tails of Anwar himself, who was then deputy PM and finance minister. Tong was the former owner of the Phileo Allied Group, an aggressive financial concern that entered the stockbroking sector in the early 1990s and quickly made a name for its deal-making abilities. In a country where politics and business are closely intertwined, the brash Tong never failed to pepper the conversations he had with local and foreign personalities in the financial sector with stories that reflected his closeness to not only Anwar, but also to Abdul Murad Khalid, a senior executive at the central bank, Negara. Banking licences are strictly controlled in Malaysia, and Tong would display his clout in 1995 when he put together a creative deal to bundle an insolvent bank, which was then under the supervision of Negara, with a one-branch Malaysian unit of Singapore's United Overseas Bank Ltd, to create Phileo Allied Bank.

The deal inspired admiration for Tong's political pull, but it also made him a target. Tong was very open about his disdain for the country's close-knit financial sector, which regarded him as an upstart, never one to shy away from reminding his adversaries about his powerful connections with Anwar and Negara's Abdul Murad, who at the time was widely regarded as one of the most powerful regulators at the central bank. He sometimes took things too far. In September 1995, a blight of a scandal hit when Tong tried

to broker a sale of stock in a troubled, publicly listed entity known as Ayer Molek Rubber Company for Negara. But the deal unravelled badly. The putative buyer, a publicly listed entity called Insas Bhd, had strong ties to the prime minister of the day, Mahathir, and Insas alleged in a police complaint that Tong had conspired with Abdul Murad to cheat the company in the deal. Tong then got into a scrap with the country's stock exchange authorities and sued the watchdog agency, only to later settle the dispute out of court.

When Anwar fell out with Mahathir in September 1998, and was replaced as finance minister by Daim Zainuddin, senior government officials, politicians, and corporate personalities aligned to the troubled politician were hounded by Mahathir and Daim. Both Tong and Abdul Murad came under investigation by the authorities for the financial deals the two had been directly involved in, and were also subjected to income tax audits.

A year after Anwar was deposed, Abdul Murad was charged with breaching the country's banking laws, for failure to disclose shares and property valued at over MYR 24 million, held in a company allegedly used by Tong as part of a fund-raising machine for Anwar's political activities. Weeks after the charge was laid came the disclosure of a startling confession by Abdul Murad, that the Anwar camp had raised over MYR 3 billion (roughly USD 789 million at the prevailing exchange rates), largely through deals in which Anwar had used his influence as the head of the national treasury. The claims were contained in a statutory declaration, a legally binding document in Malaysia, but they never amounted to much and were largely seen as a ploy to smear Anwar ahead of a national election that Mahathir would call

a month later. Tong was forced to sell his financial assets and decided to settle down temporarily in Canada. He retained a few small businesses in Malaysia, including a weekly financial publication called *The Edge*.

After Mahathir announced that he would be retiring from politics and handing over the PM's reins to his deputy, Abdullah Ahmad Badawi, Tong began preparing his return to corporate Malaysia. But Malaysia's political landscape had become very unpredictable. Anwar's release in 2004 once again made Tong a person of interest, but the businessman chose to lie low. When Najib took over in 2009, Tong became slightly more emboldened and began establishing ties with both sides of the political spectrum. He kept in close contact with Nurul Izzah, Anwar's daughter, to maintain a line with the opposition.

To ingratiate himself with people who only saw him as Anwar's avowed crony, Tong had to work hard. He was forced to be friendly with anti-Anwar operatives that had targeted him previously. He then tried to get close to Najib, a decision that first showed promise but later delivered ugly consequences. Tong lobbied hard to get a printing licence for a national daily newspaper, a luxury reserved only for political parties and businesses close to government. Najib agreed but later told Tong that he had changed his mind after two rival newspaper groups raised serious objections over Tong's previous political ties to Anwar. Spurned, Tong threw his support behind Muhyiddin and directed *The Edge* to pursue the 1MDB story. The interests of a set of disparate groups that had one common enemy, PM Najib, were starting to align.

13

The Sideshow Conspiracy 2015

In early 2015, politics in Malaysia was starting to percolate again.

Opposition leader Anwar Ibrahim was becoming a serious thorn to the embattled Najib Abdul Razak government. The federal court, Malaysia's highest judicial authority, was set to deliver its judgement on Anwar's appeal against his conviction by the Appeals Court in 2015 over charges of sexual misconduct. The judgement was to be delivered in February, and many in the Anwar camp knew the federal court, packed with judges hostile to the opposition, would uphold the conviction.

But the prospect of returning to jail did not deter Anwar, who began speaking of widespread corruption in government at nightly public engagements nationwide. He focused on the staggering debt burden created by the PM's economic brainchild, 1Malaysia Development Bhd, which had just missed a USD 563 million repayment (about MYR 2.19

billion) in a bridging loan that had come due in December. Anwar also began to annoy the Najib camp with his repeated diatribes on the abuse of power in government, particularly over the murder of a Mongolian model-turned-interpreter by two policemen who were part of Najib's security detail.

In early February, and as expected, the court upheld Anwar's conviction and five-year jail sentence. Anwar was once more imprisoned. Soon after, political chatter that centred on the PM's fraying ties with his deputy, Muhyiddin, began to gain more traction, amid speculation that Mahathir Mohamad had secretly aligned himself with the anti-Najib forces. This growing faction featured several heavy-hitters in government, including Abu Kassim Mohamed, then the chief commissioner at the Malaysian Anti-Corruption Commission (MACC), and Abdul Gani Patail, the country's Attorney General. Both civil servants had less than stellar records and they were dogged by controversy. In fact, rather than prosecuting, they were known more for covering up cases.

The plotters behind the budding coup against Najib were formidable, and businessman Tong Kooi Ong, who by this time had thrown his lot behind Muhyiddin, was desperate to be grafted. Using poker parlance, Tong needed a buy-in. Just weeks earlier, the businessman had received word that Tony Pua of the opposition Democratic Action Party (DAP) could get his hands on material that could implicate and seriously hurt Najib and 1MDB.

Tong had been told that Anwar's daughter, Nurul Izzah, had been approached to lead the charge with that material, but the terms she had suggested were rejected. Tong declared his interest and told Pua to get the broker of the stolen material to contact him. Within days, Tong received a call from Clare Rewcastle Brown of *Sarawak Report*, and soon

the major parties—including the one who held the stolen material, rogue IT executive Xavier Andre Justo—would arrange to meet in Singapore. The meeting in mid-February at the Fullerton Bay Hotel, a major landmark in Singapore that used to be the headquarters of the island state's postal system, sowed the seeds of a separate conspiracy within one of the biggest and most complex scandals to ever hit the global financial system.

In attendance were:

- Justo, the rogue IT executive, failed blackmailer, and now international smuggler of stolen confidential corporate data. He came with one goal—convince his potential buyer that the data was authentic, get his money, and get out. There was nothing altruistic.
- Brown, playing the broker, was keen to get her hands on a new story to latch on to. All she wanted was access to the data that Justo was peddling. She was in for the glory, and a story that would bring renewed relevance to her *Sarawak Report* blog, but her role would become more complicated.
- Finally, there were the buyers: Tong and his lieutenant Ho Kay Tat, who was publisher of The Edge Media Group. Were they there to expose a major scandal or get their hands on information to be used by their new patrons in a campaign to weaponize 1MDB?

At the first meeting on 15 February, the parties reached a broad agreement. Justo, however, did not quite get what he wanted. The asking price of USD 3 million was negotiated down to USD 2 million, which Justo grudgingly agreed to.

The other elements of the proposed deal were a little more curious. Brown would publish stories on her *Sarawak Report* platform, based on the stolen material, to attack Najib's government. But whatever she sought to publish had to be approved by Tong and Ho. Tong was paying, so he was dictating. The parties would meet again on 23 February at the same venue in Singapore, where Justo would spend time with Tong's IT specialists to show them how to navigate the stolen data before the agreement could be sealed. On the letterhead of Justo Consulting Co Ltd, Tong and the former PetroSaudi executive signed what may be described as a fraudulent invoice for USD 2 million in return for a non-existent IT software. But payment would soon become an issue and the deep distrust among the parties would surface.

Sarawak Report's Brown figured she had to have first bite at the story. After all, she had brought Justo and Tong together. She also did not like the way she was being dictated to by Tong and Ho, who were adamant about having the final say on what could be published. Five days after Tong and Justo inked their deal, disguised as a 'Sale of Justo Property IT Software', Brown's *Sarawak Report* blog published details of the sleazy financial dealings between 1MDB and PetroSaudi, citing company emails and documents.

The report quickly triggered chatter that someone linked to the Muhyiddin-Mahathir camp had purchased the stolen material Justo was hawking, and Brown was being tapped to ignite media attention to 1MDB and Najib. In the Najib circle, investigations would quickly centre on the boss of The Edge Media Group, Tong. There was no proof. Their suspicion was driven by the fact that publications and internet news sites under the media group's control had suddenly become more

than infatuated with the 1MDB story. All of this spooked both Tong and Ho. They quickly ceased all contact with Brown and Justo, who had yet to receive his money from the sale of the stolen data.

Distrust among the parties is to quickly set in, as Justo becomes more and more agitated over Ho's radio silence. It would be three weeks after Brown's story appears in *Sarawak Report* before Ho reaches out to Brown.

In a text message between her and Justo, Brown gripes that Ho is complaining that 'lots of people seem to know' about the stolen data. 'I have told no one, but he is insinuating that I have. He is a bit of a pain but I think his boss will deliver. If not, I will absolutely tell our mutual contact, who is Tony Pua (of the opposition DAP).'

Justo, initially confident that Ho was genuine, begins to lose faith. Additionally, he has promised money to other parties, who are waiting to collect. 'I need my money soon. I have done my duty and more,' retorts an increasingly desperate Justo, who repeatedly asks for Tong's contact details. Brown tells Justo that the boss of *The Edge* wants 'as little trace as possible', suggesting that Tong wants to keep all deliberations and actions at arm's length for self-preservation. But Tong and Ho know that breaking off all contact with Brown and Justo could force the latter two to go public.

Ho moves to set up another chat group, tagged MEET, with Brown and Justo, to help soothe frayed nerves. But the animosity between the parties spills into the open. Ho assures everyone that the agreement to pay Justo will be honoured, on condition that Rewcastle Brown stops her frolics and agrees not to publish 'sensitive' material without seeking prior consent from *The Edge* duo. 'I cannot stress enough on

this and I hope she does not take it lightly and go on her high horse and lecture me about her journalistic blah blah blah,' writes Ho, who then revises the payment deal. 'Our lives are at stake,' Ho says in a text, adding that if Brown plays her part, Justo will receive payment, with a first tranche of USD 500,000, and the rest in similar amounts, spread out between May and September. 'We have been put at risk. I am not exaggerating Clare . . . I have a 16yr old daughter whose safety I am very worried for,' Ho texts.[6]

Brown then privately expresses to Justo her disdain for Ho. 'We are dealing with a little person taking advantage of his boss, who is trying to distance himself,' she tells Justo. The chat group conversations stretch through late May, and all parties stay together to avoid being exposed. But things get mercenary and ugly as Justo becomes more desperate for his money. After consulting with Brown, and getting Tong's cell phone number from her, Justo sends this message in late April:

> Dear Mr Kooi. I use this channel instead of your email because it's safer for you. It's been a while since we met and since we agreed on what you owe me. I have been patient enough but now the situation is unbearable. It has affected my financial situation as I have been obliged to pay from my own money the people that helped me in getting the material that changed the destiny of your country. Worse than that, it has affected my personal life. I gave you the file without being paid and by doing so I betrayed the word that I gave to my wife. I have opened another account as

---

[6] https://ninequestionsforsarawakreport.blogspot.com/2015/12/breaking-details-of-justo-v-tong-ho-and.html

> you refused the first one. But this account must receive the money before the end of next week or it will be closed. I therefore urge you to pay what is due to me and by doing so respect our agreement and be a man of your word. I gave you the file without waiting for the payment because you told me that you are a man that can be trusted and we [shook] hands to confirm the agreement. This is for me the most important. But now it's the [*sic*] time to fulfil your part please. I can no longer wait or I will be in deep trouble. I don't want to threaten you, it's not who I am. But I will not let that go without fighting and if that means causing you big troubles it will be your responsibility. So please recognise that I have delivered what was agreed and that we have [succeeded] in stopping the commission machine and the people running it. Let [us] ends [*sic*] this in a proper and moral way. Thanks for confirming [to] me that you are going to pay as agreed.

Justo's note, with its thinly veiled threat, helps reopen the payment talks, but *The Edge* duo would soon tell Brown that they are worried about making any direct payment to Justo. Ho suggests devising a scheme so settlement for the purchase of stolen corporate data may be done through a third party. But that plan, which includes using bank accounts related to Brown's *Sarawak Report* and another vehicle called the Bruno Manser Fund, would collapse.

Sometime in the third week of May, Ho texts Justo directly. 'Would you be OK if it is cash? You make several visits to place of previous meetings over the next several months and you get cash.' In an immediate response, Justo texts in reply: 'Are you joking or insane?' Furious that he is being strung along, Justo shoots off a missive to Tong.

> Hello, I'm copying Ho Kay Tat and Clare. As your number 2 is proposing an unacceptable solution I'm writing to you directly. The intermediary is in Dubai, expecting the payment today or tomorrow at latest. They will leave end of the week and it will be done. If you don't pay now [I] have to assume that you don't want to pay me. By not paying me you are putting my family in big troubles! I have paid some money to the people that helped me in this deal. I will not repeat all the facts, apparently you don't care. By not honouring your word you are destroying my life. Be sure I will do the same to you! All of this started because PS [PetroSaudi] refused to pay me what was agreed when I left! They didn't think I could go so far! I'm pretty sure they are regretting it now! Do you think I will give up all of this and just walk away? I have and always will do the things I feel are right and fair! Believe me if you don't send my 2 millions before Wednesday I will use my contacts to have your PM and his lovely wife know about what you have planned! I will add some facts to be sure the sedition act applies to you and your assistant! I never wanted this, you are doing this to yourself! So please consider what you have just read and act accordingly! The decision is yours!

Amid all this wrangling, Brown continues to write stories using the stolen data, and the dispatches are also used in one form or another in publications and news sites owned by *The Edge*. Ho does not change his do-nothing approach and Justo is strung along, promised one scheme after another to effect payment by the duo from *The Edge*. But it is clear that they are afraid of any money trail. 'It's just the way to do it without putting me and my boss at risk . . . people in

Malaysia talk. I can tell you I was shocked when a good friend from an embassy here said to me, "I heard the info was sold for 2 million!!!" I was shocked and that scared the hell out of me,' Ho texts Brown.

But the warring factions don't know that PetroSaudi is planning a full-blown pushback. The company has engaged private investigators who are tracking Justo and his movements. His world is about to collapse.

In the first week of May, PetroSaudi files a report with the Royal Thai Police, alleging the attempted blackmail carried out by Justo. More than one month passes before the Southern Bangkok Criminal Court from the Samui provinces issues a warrant of arrest for the former Swiss IT executive. On 22 June 2015, the Royal Thai Police raid Justo's home, and seize computers, hard drives, assets, and phones. Justo is arrested, triggering panic among the parties who will come to be seen as thieves and smugglers of corporate-confidential data.

14

The Empire Strikes Back

By early March 2015, Prime Minister Najib Razak was beginning to feel the heat. The questions swirling around 1Malaysia Development Bhd (1MDB) were making everyone in the PM's office more than uncomfortable, and 1MDB was becoming the buzzword for all that was wrong in his government. Former PM Mahathir Mohamed's direct calls for Najib to resign because of the deepening troubles at 1MDB became more frequent, and Mahathir was taking the lead in the attack on the state fund.

Other than Mahathir's missiles, the first unexpected salvo came from Najib's deputy, Muhyiddin, during an early March cabinet meeting at which a rough outline of the troubles at 1MDB was tabled. Najib brushed off Muhyiddin's concerns, stressing that the problems at 1MDB were being exaggerated by the likes of blogger Clare Rewcastle Brown and the Malaysian business publication, *The Edge*, owned by businessman Tong Kooi Ong. But some of the issues Muhyiddin raised, although far from detailed, very much outlined the trouble at the troubled sovereign fund.

Najib discussed the issues with Arul Kanda Kandasamy, 1MDB's recently appointed chief executive officer. Arul Kanda had been brought in to supervise an elaborate corporate plan to get 1MDB back on its feet, which involved injections of property portfolios and disposal of its power-generating assets. Arul Kanda was affable, a Malaysian with Sri Lankan roots who studied law in the UK and worked in corporate finance in the Gulf states. He told Najib that Muhyiddin's summary of the troubles at 1MDB very much reflected the briefing the CEO had given to Johari Abdul Ghani, Najib's deputy minister at the finance ministry, days earlier. The circle of people Najib could trust in the government was getting smaller.

In Malaysia's hyperactive political rumour mill, talk began to spread that Zeti Aktar Aziz, the governor of Bank Negara, Malaysia's central bank, had joined the civil service cabal that Muhyiddin had formed. Standing firm with the deputy to force Najib out of office were Attorney General Abdul Gani Patail and Abu Kassim Mohamed, the chief of the Malaysian Anti-Corruption Commission (MACC).

About the same time, Low Taek Jho informed Najib that Zeti and her husband, Tawfiq Ayman, had cut all communications with him for no clear reason. Low's message confirmed that Zeti had turned, but both he and Najib could never pin down what the Muhyiddin side had on the governor. Was it her involvement in some illicit deals, or Tawfiq's close ties with Low and allegations the governor's husband had received kickbacks? In any case, Najib's political operatives would soon establish that the coup plotters were very advanced in building their case against the PM. They had surreptitiously established a special task force, comprising

top officials from the Attorney General's office, the anti-corruption agency, police, and Negara.

Also, with Zeti now part of the team, the anti-Najib forces were quickly getting the full picture of the funds flowing from 1MDB. Negara demanded local and foreign financial institutions that were facilitating 1MDB to provide full disclosure on all transactions involving the sovereign fund. In mid-March, Najib received a letter from Zeti about the troubles and alleged misappropriation of funds at 1MDB, which she claimed was part of the findings of an internal supervisory team, following an alert to the central bank by an unidentified foreign regulator.

The PM was both puzzled and bemused. His top officer at the central bank was very much in the loop, as far as he was concerned. The complex 1MDB-related flow of money had all been approved by Negara and Zeti. He did not respond to the letter. Clearly there was a high-level conspiracy against the PM. The question was: What could possibly be the end game of the coup plotters?

Then came an ultimatum from Mahathir, who had by this time sharply stepped up his public slagging of Najib. Mahathir repeatedly branded Najib a thief. Abdul Azeez Abdul Rahim, a one-time car salesman whose rough-at-the-edges character made him an ideal pit bull for Najib, came to his boss with some troubling news. He had been summoned by Mahathir, who wanted a message conveyed to Najib. Mahathir's message was pointed: There was ample proof about the wrongdoings at 1MDB. To avoid being charged, Najib simply had to step down, and a new government headed by Muhyiddin and Mahathir would make sure that no harm came to him or his family.

This was becoming Najib's very own ides of March, and the PM huddled with political advisors and his influential wife, Rosmah, and resolved there was no reason to resign. The powers that came with the prime ministership made him practically unassailable and Najib had full control of the ruling UMNO party that had set the national political agenda since independence. It was still three years away to the next general election. The plan to resolve the problems at 1MDB was already in place. He just needed to ride out the political turbulence.

When it became clear that Najib was not going to budge, his foes decided to turn up the heat. The media campaign initiated by Tong, the media group he owned and the Sarawakian blogger was also beginning to attract other local and regional publications as well as news websites, all thriving on leaks from sources within the Najib government. *The Wall Street Journal* would start to latch on to the story, its information coming from investigators involved in an ongoing Malaysian government probe, and its reports would disturb both Brown and Justo. Justo figured that Tong and his feisty chief lieutenant, Ho Kay Tat, who were giving excuse after excuse for failing to pay for the stolen data, were now directing themselves to the US publication for help to expose Najib, and other regional media companies were joining the feeding frenzy. Brown, who felt she had done most of the heavy lifting in the media campaign, was getting increasingly annoyed about being left out of the circle of anti-Najib forces.

Amid all the attacks in the media about 1MDB and calls by Mahathir for Najib to resign, pressure also began to pile up on the PM to send a strong signal to his powerful adversaries,

who were led by Mahathir and Muhyiddin. Low and his pals at PetroSaudi decided that they would weigh in.

In June 2015, Justo's arrest by the Thai police triggered panic among the parties that would come to be seen as thieves and smugglers of corporate-confidential data. For the coup plotters, there was no time to waste. They had to raise the ante, go for broke, make public what the still-secret multi-agency task force had discovered. The stage was being set for what would become the most serious face-off between rival elite factions in Malaysia's political, civil, and business worlds.

In early July 2015, *The Wall Street Journal* ran a news scoop. The report focused on Malaysian investigators scrutinizing 1MDB and how they had tracked the movement of nearly USD 681 million, held in foreign jurisdictions by companies related to the state-owned investment fund. That money, *The Wall Street Journal* reported, had found its way into Najib's personal accounts at Malaysia's AmBank during September 2013. Muhyiddin quickly seized on the sensational news and publicly broke ranks with his boss. Claiming that the report had seriously damaged Malaysia's international image, he called for an immediate probe into Najib's private accounts. Within hours of Muhyiddin's statement, Attorney General Gani Patail, a controversial advocate who had been implicated in a number of bribe-taking episodes and was known more for covering up cases than prosecuting them, would confirm to the media that he had received documents linked to the allegations of money flowing into Najib's personal accounts. The documents had come from a special task force, comprising the police, the MACC, and the central

bank, which had been set up to take further action. Battle lines were drawn.

With Najib now on the backfoot, the next challenge for the coup plotters was how to go for the jugular. The transfer of power in Malaysia since independence in 1957 has always been peaceful, and only conducted through UMNO. Not only did the party dominate every coalition government since independence, its top two leaders had also traditionally assumed the position of PM and DPM. The stumbling block for the plotters was the fact that Najib had full control of UMNO.

The special task force probe had uncovered an array of financial irregularities at 1MDB and its associate companies. The probe had uncovered business arrangements with a host of international entities and suspicious movements of funds into private accounts in tax havens that shielded the identities of the ultimate beneficiaries of the illicit financial flows. But building a case against Najib over the transactions at 1MDB would take much time, because it would have to involve getting the co-operation of agencies and governments in foreign jurisdictions, tracking down bankers, lawyers, and financial executives who had facilitated the alleged fraud and ensuring that the coup plotters, like Negara governor Zeti, did not get implicated. What was needed was evidence of a clear-cut criminal blunder that offered Najib no wiggle room.

Apart from the USD 681 million, which came from Singapore-based Falcon Bank, as reported by *The Journal*, a separate amount of MYR 42 million (about USD 12 million at the prevailing exchange rates) had also found its way into the PM's accounts at AmBank, and this time it was from domestic sources.

The source of that MYR 42 million was an entity called SRC International Sdn Bhd. Originally incorporated as a wholly owned subsidiary of 1MDB, ownership of SRC was subsequently transferred to the Ministry of Finance, which Najib headed. SRC received a MYR 4 billion loan from a state-controlled pension fund called KWAP, which was also supervised by Najib. Like 1MDB, SRC was touted by the Najib government as a strategic investment vehicle aimed at generating multiplier effects for the economy. In reality, and just like 1MDB, SRC was a political slush fund enterprise for the PM. AG Gani had found the elusive misstep that would nail Najib and force him out of office. Monies from SRC International would first flow into several other closely associated corporate vehicles, including entities controlled by Low, before ending up in Najib's personal account. The paper trails, despite the lame efforts to hide them, exposed Najib to a number of potential charges, ranging from bribery, criminal breach of trust, and money laundering. The pieces were nicely falling into place for Najib's coup plotters and time was of the essence.

The third week of July was shaping up to be one of the most crucial weeks in Malaysian politics, but it was also the least reported on. For those in the know, who counted among my network of sources, it would show how the country's political machine was concentrated in the hands of a few elite groups, democracy be damned. They would act out their own personal rivalries and ambitions in a tale of back-room machinations, manoeuvring, betrayal, deal-making, and deceit.

It all began on July 22, a Wednesday, when MACC officers picked up Rosman Abdullah, the executive chairman

of Putrajaya Perdana Bhd, a publicly listed entity that was part of Low's stable of Malaysian companies. Rosman was not in Najib's inner circle and his detention went unnoticed until he was released the following day after being held overnight for questioning. Rosman had pleaded with his captors that he needed to spend time with his family and promised to return on Friday to the anti-corruption headquarters in the administrative capital of Putrajaya, some 37 kilometres from Kuala Lumpur. The free man wasted no time before he spilled the beans to insiders in the Najib circle. Rosman told them he had been quizzed for hours about how funds from SRC international had flowed into Putrajaya Perdana through a circuitous route before the money found its way to Najib's private account in AmBank. He also told Najib's political operatives that he was being pressured give up Najib or face corruption charges. It would be the first time the Najib camp would realize that his adversaries, led by his deputy, Muhyiddin, were planning the most audacious political plot to remove him. But the 'how' remained unclear.

While they saw clearly that Muhyiddin had the backing of AG Gani, MACC boss Abu Kassim, and Negara's Zeti, the people in Najib's inner circle were unsure who else had a hand in the slowly unravelling plot. The other obvious candidate was the country's Inspector General of Police, Khalid Abu Bakar. But Najib's camp held back from contacting him, not knowing his allegiances, and things became increasingly tense for them.

It is the early hours of 25 July, a Friday. Najib is celebrating his sixty-second birthday. Shortly after gratefully accepting birthday wishes from his closest operatives, Najib places an urgent call to his home minister, Ahmad Zahid Hamidi,

who is the PM's most trusted politician in the government and UMNO. Najib informs Ahmad Zahid that he wants a team of the most loyal police personnel to pick up Putrajaya Perdana's managing director, Rosman Abdullah, and place him under police protection until further notice. Najib also instructs Ahmad Zahid that Rosman should by no means be released to the MACC.

Just before the crack of dawn, a police team arrives at Rosman's home in Kuala Lumpur and scurries him to a holding room in the national police headquarters. It is just before the break for the obligatory Friday prayers that MACC officers discover Rosman is no longer in their custody. An ugly confrontation takes place between the two agencies for Rosman, but the police will not budge. In the meantime, Najib has asked to see AG Gani and police chief Khalid for a meeting on 1MDB-related matters. The country's chief prosecutor informs the PM that investigations are proceeding smoothly and there is nothing new to report. IGP Khalid initially says nothing. But shortly after, Gani, who suffers from kidney problems, excuses himself from the meeting to make a dialysis appointment at a private clinic, and Khalid tells Najib about the plot to force him to resign at the following week's cabinet meeting.

AG Gani is to attend that cabinet meeting, typically held every Wednesday, with a readied charge sheet against the PM that would leave him with no choice but to resign and negotiate a deal with the coup plotters. Khalid tells Najib the MACC will force Rosman to provide the agency with a confession that implicates Najib, in exchange for being charged with a lesser crime.

While Najib's coup plotters remained unaware that the PM was fully briefed on what was to come at the cabinet

meeting, another crisis unfolded. Shortly after Rosman was picked up by police officers from his home on Friday, *The Straits Times* of Singapore published an exclusive interview with Justo, who, at the time was sitting in a Bangkok jail awaiting the sentence for blackmail and theft of corporate data. Justo, who had been arrested a month earlier, admitted in the interview that the media campaign against 1MDB and the Najib government, which had begun months earlier in the *Sarawak Report* and The Edge Media Group, was based on information he had stolen from PetroSaudi years earlier. Tong was not named in the first report, because he had yet to respond to *The Straits Times* queries about his involvement. Just like in 1998, when he was caught in the cross hairs of Mahathir's confrontation with Anwar Ibrahim, which forced Tong into self-exile in Canada for several years, Tong found himself in another political imbroglio. Would Muhyiddin and Mahathir provide him with protection from the Najib camp?

Faced with very limited options, Tong and his chief lieutenant decided to go on the offensive. In a nutshell, the duo threw Justo under the proverbial bus. In a joint public statement in response to the bombshell *ST* report, Tong and Ho admitted they had taken possession of the stolen PetroSaudi data. 'Justo is obviously an angry man, and understandably so, as we did not pay him what he wanted. Yes, we misled him. But that was the only way to get hold of the evidence to expose how a small group of Malaysians and foreigners cheated the people of Malaysia of US$1.83 billion.'[7] The statement was nothing

---

[7] 'The Edge owner and editor admit they 'misled' Justo over S$2.74m payment for stolen data', TODAY, 24 July 2015, https://www.todayonline.com/world/asia/edge-owner-and-editor-admit-they-misled-justo-over-s274m-payment-stolen-data.

short of stunning from an established publishing group. Here was the owner and its editorial boss openly acknowledging to breaking several cardinal rules of journalism. What's more, both *The Edge* and *Sarawak Report* blog had strung their readers along into believing that their reports were based on their own investigations, when it was actually based on stolen data from Justo, who was now wallowing in jail. Tong had little choice. He had become an accessory to the crime of data theft after signing the agreement with Justo. The only way out was to dump Justo.

As the media kerfuffle played out, Muhyiddin, Mahathir, MACC's Abu Kassim, and AG Gani would regroup to decide on the next move to counter the setback suffered when they lost control of Putrajaya Perdana's Rosman, their key witness in the Get Najib campaign. Muhyiddin and Mahathir were assured by the senior civil servants that they would get their hands on Rosman over the weekend and secure his confession, before moving on with the plan to confront Najib at the upcoming ministerial meeting on Wednesday.

Mahathir was chuffed that everything was going according to plan. Saturday, 25 July, was a big day for Mahathir, who had turned ninety on July 10. He was being feted by his business friends at a grand black-tie dinner party, themed along the James Bond movie *Skyfall*, at a major hotel in the Kuala Lumpur CBD. The shindig was organized by his favourite crony businessman, Vincent Tan Chee Yioun. It was clearly a pre-celebration to the anticipated political drama of the week that was to follow. As far as Mahathir was concerned, Najib was going to be history by the middle of that coming week and he would once again be in the driver's seat, running Malaysia together with Muhyiddin. When he was asked by reporters at the event whether he had any birthday message

for Najib, who at the time appeared to be drowning in the 1MDB quicksand, Mahathir said: 'I hope he gets to retire peacefully and enjoys his retirement.'

What Mahathir and the other coup plotters did not know was that a counter-offensive was under way. The Najib side had resolved that AG Gani had to be sacked. But, under the country's constitutional monarchy, removing a sitting AG required the consent of Malaysia's king. Najib had good relations with the palace and the green light was not a problem. But the administrative nitty-gritty had to be executed by the head of the civil service, who at the time was Ali Hamza. Ali, who held the post of chief secretary of the government, had left for a short holiday in London on Friday. As soon as he landed at Heathrow Airport, he received direct instructions from Najib that he had to take the next available flight back, or a private jet would be made available.

By early Monday (27 July), Najib was again in full control. AG Gani received a call at the start of business, from his immediate superior in the civil service, chief secretary Ali, that he had to make himself available immediately. Gani told him he was attending a conference at a hotel in KL and Ali suggested that he stay put. Ali went to the hotel and gave Gani his marching orders and both made their way back to the AG's chambers in Putrajaya under heavy police escort. Gani was ordered to clear his desk. Along with the plot to remove Najib, Gani himself was done for. When Mahathir received word about Gani's termination from office, he rested back into his reclining chair. 'I did not see this coming.'

15

State of Chaos

The sacking of Attorney General Gani Patail was the first decisive move Prime Minister Najib Razak had taken since the first of attacks against him over the growing fiasco at 1Malaysia Development Bhd (1MDB). A day after Gani's unceremonious axing on 27 July, Najib's government announced that a former judge from Malaysia's highest judicial bench, the Federal Court, would replace him with immediate effect. Mohamed Apandi Ali was, at best, considered average as a legal force by his judicial peers, as well as the lawyers who had appeared before him. But he was a loyalist to the ruling UMNO party and had long harboured political ambitions of his own. Najib knew this and was confident that Apandi would do the necessary. Under the Malaysian Constitution, the AG was not only the principal legal advisor to the government. As chief public prosecutor, Apandi held sole discretion to institute, conduct, or discontinue proceedings on any criminal offence. With Apandi's appointment, Najib no longer had any reason to worry about any legal repercussions. It was now time to quell the putsch once and for all.

On 29 July, a Wednesday, the purge against the plotters expanded. Najib dropped his deputy, Muhyiddin, and three other ministers in a cabinet reshuffle. Ahmad Zahid Hamidi, Najib's most loyal political servant who already occupied the powerful portfolio of the Home Ministry that oversees the police and other security agencies, was elevated as Deputy Prime Minister. New AG Apandi disbanded the 1MDB investigating task force his predecessor had set up. It had comprised the AG's chambers, the central bank, the Malaysian Anti-Corruption Commission (MACC), and the national police. Apandi ruled that the agencies were free to separately carry out their individual probes, but he would have the final say on how to proceed with investigation papers. As far as Najib was concerned, the domestic assault on him over 1MDB was neutralized. All he had to do now was rein in his usurpers in Negara and MACC.

As PM and finance minister, Najib enjoyed oversight over the central bank, and he dispatched one of his senior officers to inform Negara governor Zeti that he wanted her resignation. Given her complicity in the 1MDB matter, Najib figured that the central bank chief would surrender meekly and request some kind of graceful exit—perhaps a corporate-related appointment post-resignation, to salvage her reputation. He knew of the handmaiden role she played in the 1MDB affair, her dealings with Low, and how she facilitated the 1MDB deals and other related transactions, including the monies that were credited directly into his personal bank account. The plotters were careful not to leak that information to the media. But Najib was aware of much of it, and he figured Zeti would cave in easily. He did not expect what would come next.

Zeti was undecidedly haughty when she was told that Najib wanted her resignation. 'The PM will have to sack me. I intend to serve out my term,' was all she said. Najib, known to rarely lose his cool, was visibly angry, but held it in check when told about her response. He grimaced, according to one political operative who was present. But he had bigger things to worry about. How to rein in the MACC? Inspector General of Police Khalid Abu Bakar acknowledged that taking on another regulatory agency was unprecedented, but he assured Najib the police would be up to the task. However, Malaysia's police force had long lost its shine. The corruption of the system during the Mahathir years had seeped into every level of the civil service. Every branch had lost its moral compass, because Najib had encouraged what Mahathir had started. Now, Mahathir was using his influence on that same civil service to get it to revolt against a sitting PM.

The top brass at the MACC publicly declared they were not waging a political vendetta against the PM, and warned of serious consequences against any effort to suppress the ongoing 1MDB probes. Clearly, the agency had been tipped off that elements in the police were planning an operation to rein in MACC officers on grounds that they were complicit in a conspiracy to topple the government.

Four days after Gani was sacked, a crack team from the Special Branch, raided the office of Ahmad Sazilee Abdul Khairi, the MACC public prosecutor who had handled the 1MDB case and drafted the charge that was to be slapped on Najib. The crack team seized documents and the prosecutor's laptop computer. The unfolding events were unprecedented in Malaysian politics, and two of the nation's most politically powerful agencies were on a

collision course that had far-reaching consequences. Even Malaysia's military, which typically stays out of politics, was put on alert.

The country's graft-busting agency had long been considered a second-tier watchdog. It was Najib's predecessor, Abdullah Ahmad Badawi, who had decided Malaysia needed to step up its fight against corruption and had given the MACC unbridled powers by pushing through legislation just months before he would hand government to Najib in late March 2009. Previously known as the Anti-Corruption Agency, the newly minted MACC had more financial resources and muscle; it had been modelled along the famed anti-corruption commission of Hong Kong. Before long, the MACC began to distinguish itself with strong intelligence on corruption involving the police and the underworld, shady dealings between politicians and businessmen and even members of Malaysia's royalty. Soon, the agency emerged as a counter-balance to the police, including the elite Special Branch, and MACC was quickly politicized.

The police assault in the last days of July 2015 set the stage for a confrontation never seen before in Malaysia. The MACC did not have the raw muscle of the police but the damning intelligence it had quietly gathered on politicians and the country's top cops had given it serious leverage. According to Najib's close aides, the recently appointed DPM and home minister, Ahmad Zahid, was informed directly that unless the police stood down immediately, the MACC would go nuclear with its corruption findings, the implication being the whole government could be brought down.

It was something Najib could not risk. The police were ordered to stand down. Never before had an arm of government held a gun to the head of the executive. Mexican standoff, Malaysian style.

What Najib and his people did not know was that, amid all the tension, the MACC's top brass had dispatched several senior officers to provide full details of their probe to the US Federal Bureau of Investigation, which by this point had itself begun its own probe into 1MDB. The information helped the US agency fast forward the investigation process. The weaponizing of 1MDB to oust Najib at home had failed, and it was now time to internationalize a Malaysian scandal.

Low Taek Jho was getting a little anxious. After freely moving in and out at multiple US immigration check-points for years, Low was detained briefly, more than once, and questioned about his reasons for travel. What he first thought were random checks suddenly became a regular occurrence by mid-2014, particularly when travelling to New York. Clearly, he was on some US government watchlist and that could not be good. By this point, Low had built strong ties in Washington with powerful players in president Barack Obama's White House. One person in particular was Frank White Jr, a tech entrepreneur and co-founder of DuSable Capital Management, a Washington-based renewable energy and infrastructure concern. Low had nudged 1MDB to do a highly suspicious deal with DuSable that resulted in the Malaysian sovereign fund paying the US company USD 69 million in 2012. Low asked White to carry out discreet checks with top officials at the US Homeland Security agency. Word came back that the US government had been asked to keep

tabs on Low's movements by its counterpart in Malaysia. Who it was in the Malaysian government was never clear and when Low told Najib about his immigration troubles, Najib brushed it aside. The events in the final weeks of July convinced Low that both AG Gani and MACC's Abu Kassim had marked him as a person of interest for some time now. All this spelt that more trouble was on the way.

Low was not the only one starting to feel uncomfortable with Najib's political standing. The upbeat mood in Najib's inner circle after their boss moved to axe Gani Patail and drop Muhyiddin as his deputy was quickly replaced with uneasiness. There were suddenly signs, subtle but unmistakable, that things were beginning to sour. The outcome of the confrontation with the MACC was not a good sign. The MACC had changed the rules of engagement between Malaysia's political elite and a civil service that had long played a subordinate and enabling role. The relationship was now one of equals.

Zeti, who had refused to resign, was getting hot under the collar and scrambled to cover her tracks. She first ordered a full-scale investigation into AmBank and its 1MDB-related dealings. She also got Negara to seek information on the sovereign fund's cross-border money flows, particularly with banks based in Singapore. In early August, Zeti went one step further and formally presented Negara's investigation papers on 1MDB, recommending criminal action against its top management for providing the central bank with false information on the transfer of funds. AG Apandi canned the investigation papers.

In early September, senior deputy public prosecutor Anthony Kevin Morais failed to show up for work at the

AG's chambers in the administrative capital, Putrajaya, about a twenty-minute drive from KL. A reclusive lawyer of Indian descent, Morais was highly regarded as a criminal prosecutor. He was relied on heavily by his previous boss, Gani Patail. His sudden disappearance quickly sparked concern and the police were alerted.

About a week later, detectives received a crucial break when the stored-value smartcard used for toll roads, known locally as Touch 'n Go, showed up as used at a highway tollbooth some 200 kilometres outside KL. Within two days, police detained two men before rounding up five others, including an army pathologist. The authorities would also recover Morais' body at the bottom of a monsoon drain in a suburb outside KL, stuffed into an oil drum filled with concrete. The interrogation of the abductors revealed that the pathologist attached with the Malaysian Armed Forces had felt he was being unfairly targeted, and turned into a scapegoat by Morais and the AG's chambers, in a case that alleged he was running a medical-procurement swindle that also involved other senior army officers who were his superiors.

What happened was former colonel R. Kunaseegaran turned to ring-leader of a local gang, who was known to provide extortion and blackmail services for a fee. But the shakedown of Morais turned deadly. According to police investigators, six men in a Mitsubishi Triton pickup trailed Morais when he left his condominium block just before 8 a.m. on 4 September. Shortly after, they rammed his car, forcing it off the road. Two abductors shoved the small-framed Morais into the back seat of the pickup, while another pair took control of the public prosecutor's locally assembled Proton Perdana sedan and sped off in a different

direction. As Morais struggled, one of his abductors pressed his head to the floor of the vehicle and yanked his silk tie to subdue him. That yank snapped Morais' neck. He died instantly, and his abductors scrambled into a reckless plan to dispose of his body.

The gruesome murder grabbed public attention and very quickly assumed a connection to 1MDB. Morais was not directly involved in the 1MDB investigation but he was typically directed by his previous boss Gani Patail to vet legal documents and charge sheets prepared by junior public prosecutors. He worked on the case involving the SRC funds tied to Najib. Morais also initialled a correction on the draft charge sheet, a photo of which went viral on social media just before his murder.

Very quickly, speculation swirled that Morais was targeted because he himself was suspected to have leaked the draft charge sheet, and this led to another spin that drew an added link to a separate murder that took place some three years earlier.

Our story now returns to AmBank Group's founder, former Bahraini finance executive Hussain Najadi, who returned to Malaysia in 2002 after serving a prison term for crossing the royal family in his homeland.

Back in KL, Najadi struggled to get on his feet. His financial consultancy never took off and Najadi made ends meet by handling short-term assignments that came from close friends in the Malaysian banking community.

Then, the deal that had long eluded him presented itself in the form of a potential redevelopment of property that housed a Chinese temple, a stone's throw away from AmBank Group's KL headquarters. Najadi's Malaysian wife, Cheong Mei Kuen,

had strong rapport with the key trustees of the temple, who were also being wooed by two other potential bidders, namely public prosecutor Morais' younger brother, Richard, and a group of Chinese businessmen with underworld connections. Richard, who long ran a business of selling reconditioned pianos with his Chinese wife, also had links with gangsters that ran protection rackets. The Chinese businessmen saw Richard as their main competition in the land deal and put out a contract on him. A hitman nicknamed Sei Ngan Chai, or 'bespectacled boy' in the Cantonese dialect, was told that his target was an Indian man with a Chinese wife. When Najadi escorted his wife from a meeting at the temple to their vehicle in a nearby open-air carpark behind the AmBank headquarters, Sei, who had been loitering around the area, stepped up in front of the couple and shot the finance executive at close range. The three shots to the chest killed Najadi immediately. His wife, who suffered a gunshot to her leg, survived. Police ruled Najadi's killing a case of mistaken identity, but after the death of Morais, the public prosecutor, Najib's detractors quickly began spinning that Najadi's death was somehow tied to 1MDB because he had received information on the shady dealings at the bank he had founded.

There was little that the Najib camp could do to offset the increasingly toxic narrative that pummelled his already damaged political prestige. In private, Najib told his closest supporters that the bad times would pass. He reasoned that the 1MDB rationalization was moving according to plan. His legal troubles were being ironed out by his friendly AG, Appandi Ali, who had rejected Negara's recommendation to level criminal charges against 1MDB management, and instead slapped a fine of MYR 15 million on the fund.

In the meantime, Low Taek Jho, who had turned to his ties in Saudi Arabia and the UAE for the first two financial scams, set his sights on China to design an elaborate scheme to resolve the sovereign fund's looming financial commitments. Low had an impressive set of contacts among the children of several of Beijing's powerful political class. China was keen to find a strong economic partner to expand its interest in Southeast Asia and find a base where it could exert more influence over the disputed waters of the South China Sea. By early 2016, Malaysia's new China pivot had become the latest economic initiative of Najib's administration. The deals Low was putting together with Chinese entities, with the blessing of Kuala Lumpur, helped register foreign direct investment flows and turned Malaysia into the most favoured destination for mainland Chinese businesses.

By mid-2016, the Malaysian government had signed USD 34 billion worth of Chinese investments in power generation and property development, along with contract awards to build railway networks, gas pipelines, and other infrastructure projects, such as ports. In reality, these investments and projects were part of a grand scheme to bailout 1MDB. The purchases of Malaysian assets by state-owned Chinese companies were inflated in order to disguise kickbacks that flowed into a slush fund to meet 1MDB progress debt payments. Similarly, Malaysia awarded government infrastructure contracts to Chinese concerns at bloated valuations. These projects were funded by loans from state-owned banks in China, on terms that allowed for Malaysia to receive up to 80 per cent of the project-funding upfront. These funds went towards dealing with

1MDB's debt woes. Najib sidestepped any worries about the government itself creating a potential Malaysian debt trap down the road. The PM's narrative for Malaysians framed 1MDB problems as manageable, the **claims by his** detractors as politically motivated. His step now had a distinct gait. But it did not last long.

On 20 July, the US Department of Justice filed a civil forfeiture complaint seeking the recovery of over USD 1 billion in assets associated with the laundering of funds misappropriated from 1MDB.

The charge sheet alleged the following. 'From 2009 through 2015, more than $4.5 billion in funds belonging to 1MDB were allegedly misappropriated by high-level officials of 1MDB and their associates, and Low Taek Jho (aka Jho Low), through a criminal scheme involving international money laundering and embezzlement. Some of the embezzlement proceeds were also allegedly used to pay bribes. 1MDB was created by the government of Malaysia to promote economic development in Malaysia through global partnerships and foreign direct investment. Its funds were intended to be used for improving the well-being of the Malaysian people. Instead, funds held by 1MDB and proceeds of bonds issued for and on behalf of 1MDB were taken and spent on a wide variety of extravagant items, including luxury homes and properties in Beverly Hills, New York, and London; a 300-foot superyacht; and fine art by Monet and Van Gogh. The funds also were sent into numerous business investments, including a boutique hotel in Beverly Hills, a movie production company that made "The Wolf of Wall Street" while the embezzlement scheme was ongoing, the

redevelopment of the Park Lane Hotel in Manhattan, and shares in EMI, the largest private music-rights holder.'[8]

For a majority of Malaysians, the stories revolving around Najib and his cohorts over the handling of 1MDB were all true and worse. Suddenly, Najib found himself trapped in a political no-man's land. While he remained in control of government until the next general election in the first half of 2018, the prospect of him and UMNO losing power was something that could not be dismissed. The widening feeling of despair pushed the government into a period of permanent crisis.

The unending stream of disclosures of corporate skulduggery at 1MDB emboldened the political usurpers led by Mahathir. The big question now was: What could be done next? Najib had complete control of the levers of power and the ruling UMNO. Their options were limited. To dislodge Najib, Mahathir and gang would need to not only destroy the political party that had long defined stability in Malaysia, they would have to make peace with Mahathir's political nemesis—jailed opposition leader Anwar Ibrahim. What Mahathir did not realize at the time was that a desperate Najib was thinking the same thing.

---

[8] 'Justice Department repatriates $1.4B misappropriated 1MDB funds to Malaysia', IRS, 13 June 2014, https://www.irs.gov/compliance/criminal-investigation/justice-department-repatriates-1-point-4b-misappropriated-1mdb-funds-to-malaysia.

16

The Wooing of Anwar Ibrahim

It was 16 September 2016. Media crews from the print, online, radio, and television sectors had been alerted to make their way to the High Court, where an application opposing a government amendment to the country's already tough security laws was being challenged by the jailed opposition leader Anwar Ibrahim. Only a year earlier, Anwar had been found guilty on another sexual misconduct charge that had first been dismissed by a lower court, but upheld by an appellate bench on the prodding of the Najib Razak government.

Appearing at the court complex ahead of the Black Maria van that would ferry Anwar from the prison was former prime minister, Mahathir Mohamad, who made his way to greet his arch political opponent with his signature cynical smile. (The Black Maria is slang in Commonwealth nations for police or prison vehicles that transport prisoners).

Video of the encounter between the two sworn foes went viral on social media, and confirmed earlier murmurings that Mahathir had set his mind on a political comeback with

the sole intention of dislodging Najib and UMNO. Seven days prior to showing up at the court hearing for Anwar's application, Mahathir had founded a party called Parti Pribumi Bersatu Malaysia, or Bersatu, together with his son, Mukhriz, and the deposed deputy PM, Muhyiddin. All three had resigned from UMNO weeks earlier.

Bersatu brandished a hastily assembled constitution that mirrored UMNO's. But to entice ethnic Malays, the majority race in Malaysia, to abandon UMNO would require presenting a real alternative to the UMNO-led coalition government.

The only way to do it was to make peace with the sole probable ally available at the time, the Anwar-led Pakatan Harapan (PH; Alliance of Hope). The PH coalition was a motley assortment of centre-right parties that had come together in 1998 to collectively distance themselves from Mahathir after he had jailed Anwar that year. And here was the most fateful of turns: The man who had built the toxic political infrastructure that had enabled Najib to become near invincible, was now turning to political opponents he had jailed whenever they became a nuisance during the twenty-two years he held power, beginning in 1981.

Mahathir, the master of the political endgame, immediately seized the opportunities that presented themselves in this dramatic state of affairs. Najib was on the ropes. His main threat, Anwar, was incarcerated. Many young Malaysians, who were coming to voting age, knew nothing about the follies of former PM Mahathir that had brought the country to this very precarious crossroad. Mahathir set in motion the plays that would manipulate the situation to his benefit. The meeting with Anwar at the High Court that 16 September was the first move by Mahathir on

the chessboard of his comeback strategy. Anwar himself was suspicious. But many of his allies in the opposition, including Lim Kit Siang of the Democratic Action Party (DAP), the country's fiercest Mahathir critic, who was often at the receiving end of the former PM's repressive crackdowns on political opponents, argued that a détente was worth considering.

To be sure, what Mahathir was demanding was a very big ask. He wanted to lead the opposition campaign at the upcoming elections, due before the end of May 2018. Should the opposition coalition win, Mahathir wanted a guarantee that he would be appointed PM. The deep trust issues between Mahathir and the opposition leadership aside, the big question that loomed centred on how such an arrangement would sit with many ordinary Malaysians, particularly the growing middle class that had long been the support base of the opposition coalition.

Many could not bring themselves to forgive Mahathir for his autocratic ways, including the brutal ejection of Anwar after both politicians fell out in 1998. Many Malaysians also held the view that Najib had been prodded by Mahathir to join the sinister political plan to jail Anwar in 2015. Then there was the widely held, and by no means misplaced, concern over entering a deal with a slippery politician, whose proclivity to renege on deals and make plain-faced denials of any previous agreement was legendary. And so began months of backroom negotiations between Mahathir and Saifuddin Nasution Ismail, easily the only person Anwar trusted absolutely apart from his wife, Wan Azizah Wan Ismail, who led his Parti Keadilan Rakyat, or People's Justice Party. It took months of close-door talks and several confidence building

trips by Mahathir to meet Anwar at the corridors of the High Court.

While Anwar agreed to the arrangement, the trust issues with Mahathir remained palpable, especially after the latter had enticed former finance minister Daim Zainuddin out of retirement to help him shape the electoral battle plan against Najib. Daim's return troubled Anwar. He knew that the likes of Wan Azizah and Saifuddin were no match for the Mahathir-Daim team. Anwar had always believed they were the chief architects behind his ugly and brutal removal from power because they feared their corporate misdeeds would be exposed in the aftermath of the regional financial crisis that had hit in the first half of 1997. Anwar needed some other leverage. Saifuddin was both trouble-shooter and the builder of bridges for Anwar. He instructed Saifuddin to quietly open talks with Najib's chief political ally, deputy PM Ahmad Zahid Hamid, who now was also Najib's No. 2 in UMNO. While a desperate Najib was losing political ground with each passing day, and getting increasingly concerned with the inexplicable alliance between Mahathir and the Anwar-led coalition, his deputy quickly warmed to the idea presented by Saifuddin.

Within days Saifuddin and Ahmad Zahid began meeting regularly, often at the deputy PM's home in the luxurious, gated neighbourhood of Kajang Heights, some 20 miles outside KL. They met mostly after Isha, the last of five mandatory prayers Muslims perform each day. At one of those sessions, Saifuddin casually mentioned to Ahmad Zahid that Anwar was suffering from serious pain in his right shoulder, and treatment by the prison's dispensary and doctors was not enough. As Home Minister, Ahmad Zahid

immediately ordered the prison authorities to get Anwar to a government hospital in KL. After receiving medical attention and being examined there, doctors recommended immediate surgery, which the Najib government did not oppose. The surgery went well and Najib and Ahmad Zahid decided to go public with their courting of Anwar by visiting him in the hospitals. Pictures of their encounters with Anwar flooded social media and triggered intense political speculation, which in turn gave the opposition leaders greater clout in their negotiations with the Mahathir camp.

In January 2018, after more than a year of backroom negotiations that Anwar guided from behind the scenes, a deal was reached between the Anwar and Mahathir camps. Anwar was named leader of the opposition coalition, Pakatan Harapan (PH), with Mahathir as chairman and Anwar's wife, Wan Azizah, president. Under the deal, Mahathir would assume the position of interim PM should PH succeed in toppling Najib and his National Front coalition. Mahathir also made a commitment that he would immediately set in motion a process to secure a royal pardon for Anwar and pass the leadership baton to him. No time frame was specified publicly but the general thinking was that one year would be enough for Mahathir, who at the time was already ninety-two years old. The deal looked good on paper, but Anwar, who by this time had been on the receiving end of Mahathir's political perfidy countless of times, remained suspicious, his support tentative, and figured it best to let things play out before making the next move.

Amid all the uncomfortable sentiments percolating in the opposition camp, the Anwar-Mahathir détente was nothing short of a game changer for Malaysian politics. The distaste

that middle-ground Malaysia had for Mahathir began to slowly dissipate and many began to lean on the idea that the 'Old Man' had seen the errors of his ways and wanted to make amends. Mahathir campaigned like a man possessed. He criss-crossed the nation to address well-attended rallies and delivered scathing attacks against Najib over the 1MDB affair and the PM's free-spending wife, Rosmah Mansor, notorious for her extravagant jewellery and handbags. Traction began to build in the Malay heartland, the bedrock of support for UMNO and Najib. Soon UMNO's own internal surveys were showing that the Malays were beginning to contemplate the unthinkable: voting against the political party that secured independence in 1957.

The growing prospect of the UMNO-led coalition not winning enough seats in parliament to form the next government forced Najib to explore options. Right-wing elements in UMNO were pushing Najib to lay the groundwork for declaring a state of emergency in the event the government lost power. But Najib knew that such a move would have devastating implications for Malaysia, which ranked as one of the world's top twenty trading nations. Instead, Najib assigned Ahmad Zahid to keep communication lines open with Anwar, who was given government permission to serve his jail-time in hospital. Ahmad Zahid kept in close contact with Saifuddin, who was allowed to see Anwar regularly. Saifuddin was also given a mobile phone by Ahmad Zahid, with a Thailand SIM card to avoid anyone tapping their conversations. Najib and Ahmad Zahid began to float the idea of mutual co-operation with PH in the event of a hung parliament. Anwar, who never trusted Mahathir, did not oppose the plan.

Malaysian politics was once again at a bizarre place.

17

How Power Changed Hands

It was Wednesday, 9 May 2018, and many Malaysians woke that morning to a sense that something historic could be afoot.

It was election day in Malaysia and you could feel the sentiment for change. Malaysian homes were housing returning family and friends who had left their country to set up home in Singapore, Australia, and Canada, and they had returned to make their vote count. The opposition had come very close in two previous elections; it had denied a two-thirds parliamentary majority to the long-ruling National Front coalition headed by UMNO in 2008, and snatched the popular vote for the very first time in the 2013 poll. In the opposition camp, the sentiment was that Malaysia's 13th general election since independence in 1957 would mark a new beginning. Internal surveys were showing that public sentiment had begun to shift away from both the National Front and UMNO, and change on the ground was gaining momentum as the political parties headed to the finish. To many, this was the Malaysian moment.

The rollercoaster drama would begin around 8 p.m. as social media exchanges began reporting that political bigwigs from the National Front were badly trailing their opposition rivals in initial vote counts. By 10.30 p.m., they were falling like pins and it became clear that one of the world's longest ruling governments was headed for a historic electoral defeat. Suddenly, the Election Commission, independent by constitution but pandering to every whim of Najib's administration in the run-up to the polls, adopted radio silence and did not announce the election results. It was another sign that this election was unlike any other.

The Najib camp was now in crisis mode. The popular view among National Front leaders going into the election was that the coalition would emerge with a slim majority and UMNO, as the party with the largest number of seats in parliament, would form government. But a number of leaders feared that those at the top were disconnected from ordinary Malaysians; refusing to acknowledge public sentiment towards the government was at its lowest due to the 1MDB scandal, a succession of corruption cases involving UMNO kingpins, and anger towards Najib's overbearing wife, Rosmah Mansor. But even among this group, the worst-case scenario was that the election outcome would produce no clear winner, a situation that would very likely prompt the caretaker Najib government to declare a temporary state of emergency while it cobbled together a new coalition to form government. In their collective minds, UMNO and the National Front losing power was never a possibility. By 11 p.m., close aides to Najib told him the results were showing that candidates from UMNO and its partners were faring very badly and, if the trend persisted, Malaysia could move into uncharted waters.

As despair and gloom began to build at KL's World Trade Centre, where UMNO and its supporters had gathered, it became apparent to the media that the real news was unfolding across town. Ensconced in a large function room of the Sheraton Hotel in Petaling Jaya, a satellite city of KL, Mahathir and opposition comrades opened their post-election operations room to the media. Developments at the Sheraton Hotel function room were being streamed 'live', not just on national TV but across all social media platforms, and speculation mounted that the National Front had lost the election.

The function room was seized by frenzy. Mahathir went 'live' on TV to claim that the opposition had won the election. He and other opposition leaders began to wave their mobile phones, each with a screenshot of a digital board of the operations rooms at national police headquarters that kept real-time updates of the electoral count. Within minutes, that screenshot was all over social media. The opposition coalition had taken control of 127 parliamentary seats, a comfortable majority in the 222-member lower house chamber. The National Front was trailing with only 86 seats and talk about Najib declaring a state of emergency spread like wildfire, only to be accompanied by calls on social media for Malaysians to take to the streets to defend the election results. Within the hour, many 'ordinary' Malaysians in KL would leave their homes and converge around the Sheraton Hotel. An open soccer field a stone's throw away from the hotel, which fronted one of the oldest A&W fast-food outlets in Malaysia, became the venue to assemble.

As the number of Malaysians at the soccer field grew, the nation's Conference of Rulers—nine sultans who take turns

to serve a five-year term as king under the country's unique constitutional monarchy—moved to intervene. Several sultans made direct phone calls to the heads of police and armed forces instructing the top brass to maintain order and ensure that the election results were respected.

Suddenly, Malaysia's future was in the hands of three men: Najib, a scandalous PM fighting for his political life; Mahathir, battling to keep together the flawed system he had created by cosying up to the opposition; and Anwar, who was finally seeing the fruits of his decades-old fight for reform and change. How these three would come to play the hands they were dealt would shape the coming hours and determine how the first ever transfer of power in Malaysia, from sitting government to opposition, would be accomplished.

The Election Commission was ordered by the Conference of Rulers to begin releasing official results, and broke silence to declare Malaysia's 13th general election had delivered a hung parliament. The declaration set a highly charged situation on a new trajectory that led to political horse-trading and engineered defections through financial inducements, both of which were commonplace in the Malaysian election process.

Mahathir began to sense that factions in the PH coalition were beginning to explore possibilities that did not include him. This first sign of worry was the conspicuous absence of Saifuddin Nasution, who was Anwar's chief political lieutenant from Parti Keadilan Rakyat (PKR; People's Justice Party), the dominant member in the PH coalition. Saifuddin was huddled together with Anwar at a heavily guarded government hospital room, where the jailed opposition leader had been allowed to recuperate from shoulder surgery. Anwar's lieutenant still had

the mobile phone that carried a Thai SIM card handed to him by Najib's No. 2, Ahmad Zahid. Other scenarios had to be canvassed, new outcomes negotiated. Anwar and Saifuddin were told that the Conference of Rulers was not keen to appoint Mahathir as PM.

Malaysia's Federal Constitution clearly states that the leader of the party that emerges with the largest number of parliamentary seats shall be appointed prime minister by the king to pave the way for the formation of a new government. In previous elections since 1957, this party had always been the UMNO-led National Front, a legally registered coalition with a proper leadership structure. But Malaysia was now in a political wilderness.

While the National Front was an officially recognized coalition under Malaysian law, the loosely assembled PH coalition was not. On top of that, PH was offering Mahathir, leader of its most junior member, the newly established Bersatu, as its candidate from prime minister. All of these raised several prickly legal and constitutional issues.

Sultan Muhammad V, the king, was no fan of Mahathir, and he, like many of his fellow sultans, was not keen for his return as PM. It was the early hours of 10 May 2018, and as Malaysians remained glued to their phones and TV, the palace reached out to the PH coalition with instructions that the King wanted an immediate audience with Anwar's wife, Wan Azizah Wan Ismail, who was also the president of the People's Justice Party, which prisoner Anwar was directing from his hospital bed. Mahathir was informed. He was not pleased that he was being taken out of the equation.

At the 3 a.m. audience that Thursday, the King made it clear to Wan Azizah he could not accept Mahathir's

nomination as the candidate for PM because he was not the leader of the dominant party in parliament. Wan Azizah was told it would be more acceptable if she were presented as the candidate. Meanwhile, in Wan Azizah's absence, speculation of secret deals between Najib and Anwar swirled in hushed tones at the Sheraton function room. Mahathir was told by his allies in the Special Branch that efforts were afoot within the Najib and Anwar camps to block his appointment as PM, and that this had received tacit royal approval.

But Mahathir, always the master of the endgame, was not to be defeated. In a nationally televised press conference, Mahathir declared all the elected candidates from the opposition coalition had unanimously agreed to nominate him as their prime ministerial candidate. The letter supporting his candidature was handed to the palace at 1.38 p.m. on Thursday.

Shortly after, the Election Commission handed the official results to the King. The Pakatan Harapan coalition had won. The palace asked to see Mahathir along with other coalition leaders at 5 p.m. Mahathir did not attend the meeting, but Wan Azizah led the delegation of PH alliance leaders to the palace, who all confirmed that they supported Mahathir as prime minister. It sealed the deal, and at 9.30 p.m. on 10 May 2018, Mahathir was officially sworn in as Malaysia's prime minister for the second time.

For the leaders and supporters of the National Front and UMNO, a sense of incredulity prevailed over what was happening. For Najib and his wife, Rosmah, it was nothing short of horror. The son of Malaysia's second prime minister, long considered a card-carrying member of the aristocrat class, had been summarily dismissed by ordinary Malaysians in a campaign by the same man who had helped bring him

to power. Now he worried about what Mahathir would do to him in political retribution. Flashes of what Anwar endured when he clashed with Mahathir filled the Najib home with untold anxiety.

Najib planned a quick dash to the airport that catered for tycoons with private jets. But news that he was on a flight manifest would leak and Malaysians converged at the former domestic airport in Subang to make sure he and Rosmah did not leave. Najib's battle for survival was just beginning. For Malaysia, normal was no more.

18

Under Siege

The mood among most Malaysians who voted for change was mixed. The unthinkable had just been accomplished. The political coalition that had held uninterrupted power since independence in 1957 had just collapsed. But something was just not right. Mahathir Mohamad, the architect of much of what had long troubled Malaysia, was leading the new government and there was widespread scepticism that he had changed his ways.

Xavier Andre Justo was watching developments unfold in Malaysia with great interest from his homeland in Switzerland. The disgraced fomer IT executive of PetroSaudi International was the only person to pay any kind of price for participating in the 1MDB fiasco. He was sentenced to three years in jail in a Thailand court in August 2015 after pleading guilty to blackmail, extortion, and peddling stolen PetroSaudi data. Justo observed from afar how his other fellow conspirators, blogger Clare Rewcastle Brown and Tong Kooi Ong, the publisher of Malaysian news organization, The Edge Group, were basking in

the limelight claiming that they had led the media charge of exposing the 1MDB scandal. The two had distanced themselves from Justo, who had sued Tong while in jail in the Singapore courts for the USD 2 million that he was promised. Tong refused to pay on grounds that Justo had widely confessed to stealing the PetroSaudi data.

Justo needed to lift the gloom that now surrounded his life and the changes taking place in Malaysia offered opportunities. He quickly made his way to the capital Kuala Lumpur days after Malaysia's historic May 2018 general election and shortly after secured a meeting with Mahathir, who was now premier for the second time. Justo presented himself to Mahathir as the aggrieved whistle-blower, who was instrumental in lifting the lid on the 1MDB scandal, and was seriously short-changed in the process by Tong, who strung him along over the promise of payment and dumped him after he was arrested by the Thai police. Mahathir assured Justo that he would look into the matter and promptly directed Tong to keep up with his end of the bargain over the stolen data.

But honouring the USD 2 million payment to Justo raised a number of sticky legal issues for a one-time stockbroker. Any settlement to the contract both parties had signed in February 2015 in Singapore would immediately make Tong a direct accomplice to the serious violations of data theft that Justo had been convicted for. The payment had to be disguised and it would take some trickery. All parties also needed to reach a new deal that would keep hidden the messy business of the stolen data and the wrangling over payment in the months leading to Justo's arrest in Thailand. (The reconstruction of events in Chapters 12 and 13 were based on emails and also mobile phone WhatsApp transcripts that

the Thai police had obtained when they arrested Justo at his home in the resort island of Koh Samui. The lengthy police dossier also included numerous confessions by Justo while in prison.)

Very quickly, the IT rogue was be presented to the public as the hallowed whistle-blower to the financial scandal that brought down the Najib government. Justo began appearing in radio talk shows and readily gave media interviews over the steep price he had paid in exposing the 1MDB affair together with Brown. It would take a whole eight months before Tong would enter into a financial settlement with Justo over the sale of the PetroSaudi data. It was camouflaged in media events as a gift to a whistle-blower from a grateful Malaysian businessman for the huge personal cost the Swiss national had suffered.

Tong and Justo were not the only ones trying to cover their tracks.

Sometime in mid-2019, lawyers representing fugitive financier Low Taek Jho, received a curious communication from the Singapore authorities requesting information over monies held in an offshore bank account by a little-known entity called Iron Rhapsody.

The lawyers were asked whether their client would be laying a claim on the frozen funds, estimated at just over USD 20 million, because the principal shareholder of the Iron Rhapsody account, Malaysia businessman Tawfiq Ayman, had informed the Singapore authorities that the monies were being held in trust for Low.

The funds in the Iron Rhapsody account were frozen because it was allegedly tainted by money flows tied to the 1MDB scandal. Low's lawyers informed the Singapore

authorities that the monies did not belong to their client and he did not intend to make any claim on the funds.

Tawfiq is no ordinary Malaysian. He was born Lee Ban Siew and he converted to Islam when he married Zeti Akhtar Aziz, who served as Malaysia's central bank governor between 2000 and 2016.

By this point, I had been reporting on 1MDB for just over a decade. My first notes on the subject in my personalised four-inch-by-eight-inch reporter's notepad began with something a forex trader from Negara told me over about how Zeti had made that hugely unexpected appearance at the central bank's trading room to personally instruct her officers to release the flow of the 1MDB funds to the offshore entities tied to PetroSaudi International, setting into motion easily the most storied financial scandal in Malaysian history.

How much Low had extended to Tawfiq has never been revealed. In my conversations with Low through his lawyers, the financier who remains on the run believes that it was close to USD 40 million that was handed over to his former business partner.

Nevertheless, Tawfiq would eventually surrender the funds amounting to USD 16.2 million to the Singapore government, but no action was taken against him in the island republic or back in Malaysia.

By this time, it was becoming clear that the new government had no interest in getting to the bottom of the 1MDB affair. Simply put, Mahathir could not afford a full and public accounting of the 1MDB scandal. The prime minister who sat at the top for more than two decades and came back from retirement to become PM again in 2018 was very much the architect of the political system that paved the

way for a criminal such as Najib to lie, cheat, and steal his way to power. Sadly, Mahathir's new partners in government, who were hugely critical of the shenanigans of 1MDB in the run-up to the 2018 general election, went along with his Machiavellian machinations, which in turn allowed the country's elite who enabled the world's largest kleptocracy to go unpunished. Zeti, for example, was first appointed to the top-level government economics advisory group and subsequently assigned to the prestigious position as chairman of the state-owned investment fund known as Permodalan Nasional Bhd.

Malaysia's efforts to bring back the so-called financial mastermind of the multi-layered embezzlement schemes at 1MDB, Low Taek Jho, has been feeble at best. The fugitive financier reached a settlement in 2019 with the US Department of Justice to give up more than USD 700 million in assets. He remains on the run and is widely believed to be holding out in Shanghai, China.

It was different for Najib.

Barely two months after he was ejected from power, Najib was arrested and slapped with seven charges from receiving bribes and criminal breach of trust in early July. More charges would follow and by the time government prosecutors were done with framing their cases against the former premier, Najib was facing five counts of corruption, nine counts of criminal breach of trust, and twenty-eight counts of money laundering. His trial at Malaysia's High Court, over seventy-nine days between April 2019 and March 2020, culminated with his conviction and he was sentenced to twelve years in jail and a fine of MYR 210 million. He was finally dispatched to prison on 23 August2022 after Malaysia's

Federal Court, the apex judicial body, rejected his appeals and upheld both the conviction and his sentence.

It marked the first time that a former Malaysian premier has been sentenced to jail, but that did not help settle the country's bumpy political terrain. The newly installed Mahathir government lasted only twenty-two months. It fell after Mahathir's No. 2, Muhyiddin Yassin, and his supporters staged a political coup by pulling out of the fragile coalition government and joined forces with UMNO, the party he left after falling out with Najib in 2015, to form a new government that only lasted seventeen months. UMNO's Ismail Sabri Yaakob, a seat warmer, took over as premier until a fresh general election was called in November 2022. The opposition coalition, this time led by Mahathir's chief political nemesis Anwar Ibrahim, emerged with the single-largest block of elected representatives in parliament but short of the majority needed to form government. The inconclusive election result forced Anwar to team up with UMNO to form the new government and paved the way for him to take over as premier.

Malaysian politics remains in a funk and issues surrounding 1MDB continue to percolate. Najib, with access to vast amounts of cash from his plundering nine-year reign, continues to wield major influence over UMNO and has become a persistent thorn to the Anwar government.

Malaysia remains under siege.

Afterword and Acknowledgements[9]

Many would prefer to move past the 1Malaysia Development Bhd (1MDB) scandal that has come to mirror the institutionalized political corruption in Malaysia.

But this nasty affair, which until now has been laden with selective reporting of accounts that shade the truth, continues to make news in Malaysia and beyond.

Its chief protagonist, jailed former premier Najib Razak, remains a public nuisance. He has shown no remorse, no contrition, and no shame. He claims innocence over his convictions for corruption and accuses the Malaysian judiciary of waging a vendetta against him. Under very controversial circumstances in end-January 2024, Malaysia's Pardons Board, which is headed by the King, halved Najib's twelve-year prison sentence and reduced the MYR 210 million fine to MYR 50 million. He has also initiated a legal campaign to serve out the remainder of his jail sentence under house arrest, much to the consternation of ordinary Malaysians.

[9] This book was written independently by the author without any involvement from CNA. All information, views, and opinions expressed in this book are solely those of the author and do not reflect the views or opinions of CNA.

Testimony from several witnesses, including former central bank governor Zeti Akhtar Aziz, in other ongoing 1MDB-related cases against Najib, are also producing conflicting accounts. Among the most sensational declarations in court are her outright rejection to claims that she knew Low Taek Jho. But Low has insisted that ties with the former governor and her family date back to his days at the Wharton School of the University of Pennsylvania. 'She even visited me at my UPenn apartment at 917 Chestnut Hall,' Low noted in a mobile text forwarded to me through one intermediary based in Hong Kong. 'Can you imagine if I came out to talk. She would be toast. Of course it's her word against mine and they would argue she is more credible.'

There is little doubt that *The Siege Within* will renew debate of the 1MDB debacle and will very likely intensify pressure on the government of Prime Minister Anwar Ibrahim to revisit this matter and bring details of the cover-up into the public domain. Already, the Anwar administration is considering rolling back on the settlement agreement between the Malaysian government and Goldman Sachs, a move that would clearly suggest that the shenanigans at 1MDB did not end with Najib.

The reconstruction of events in the pages of this book are based on extensive first-hand reporting and the review of documents, confidential consultant reports, internal bank audits, private emails, and government material. And this would not have been possible without the generosity of so many people who agreed to share information, insights, and access to highly sensitive material that helped put pieces of the 1MDB puzzle together. They spoke to me, allowed me access to highly sensitive material and insights on condition

they stay nameless. They include three close friends, who were given access to the original manuscript. To all of them, I am deeply grateful for their trust and the shared belief that this story needed to be told.

There are people that I would like to name.

My most sincere gratitude goes to my dear friend Indra Ramanathan. Indra sustained cajoling, sometimes bordering on being a downright nuisance, was instrumental in me finishing this project. Unfortunately, Indra left this earthly coil in January 2024, before he could see the end product. Thank you, matey. We did this together.

William de Cruz, my cousin who was involved in this project from the very start. William not only played a big role in the editing of the manuscript as it developed, but he often reminded me about the important things that required capturing in this project about a country we only know as home.

I also could not have done this without my very large family, absent and present.

And finally to my wife, Surinder, and our daughter, Nisha. Thank you for always being my lighthouse.

Cast of Characters and Institutions

In Order of Appearance

Prologue

Anwar Ibrahim
Mahathir Mohamad
Suharto
Najib Abdul Razak
Low Taek Jho
Gani Patel
Muhyiddin Yassin

The Asian Wall Street Journal
Perwaja
Malaysia Inc.
UMNO (United Malays National Organization)
1Malaysia Development Berhad (1MDB)
Goldman Sachs

Chapter 1

George Soros
Jaffar Hussein
Nor Mohamed Yackop
Zeti Akhtar Aziz
Ungku Abdul Aziz bin Ungku Abdul Hamid
Norazah Abdul Aziz
Aziz Taha
Daim Zainuddin
Ahmad Mohamed Don
Fong Weng Pak
Clifford Herbert
Aris Othman

Bank Negara aka Negara
Deutsche Bank
Price Waterhouse
PetroSaudi International

Euromoney
The Bankers
Financial Times
University of Malaya
Wharton Business School, University of Pennsylvania
South East Asian Central Banks (SEACEN) Research and Training Centre
Malaysian Finance Ministry

Chapter 2

Tajudin Ramli
Kadir Jasin
Lim Thiat Kiat
Ali Abul Hassan Sulaiman
Razali Abdul Rahman
Hasan Abas
Wan Azmi Wan Hamzah
Halim Saad

Special Branch
Malaysia Chinese Association (MCA)
United Engineers Malaysia Bhd (UEM)
Renong Bhd
New York Stock Exchange
National Economic Action Council
Multi-Purpose Group
Chase Manhattan
Amanah
Urban Development Authority (UDA)
Technology Resources Industries Bhd (TRI)
Celcom
Malaysia Airline System (MAS)
Bangkok Bank
International Commercial Bank (ICB)
Khazanah Holdings

Chapter 3

Abdullah Ahmad Badawi
Kamaluddin Abdullah
Ananda Krishnan
Khairy Jamaluddin
Eric Chia
Syed Mokhtar Albukhary
Nikolai Dobberstein
Omar Merican
Nizam Razak
Kamal Siddiqi
Yahya Ahmad

Vincent Tan Chee Yioun
Rohana Othman
Saleh Sulong
Tawfiq Ayman
Nasimuddin Amin
Kamal Khalid

National Front (Barisan Nasional)
Wynton Capital
McKenzie Consulting, Malaysia
DRB-Hicom
Heavy Industries Corp, or Hicom
Proton
Frazer-Nash
EON
Diversified Resources Bhd
Petronas, or Petroliam Nasional Bhd
Kuwait Projects Company, or KIPCO
Wynton Private Equity Group
ADKMIC, or Abu Dhabi-Kuwait-Malaysia Investment Corp
Swan Symphony
Autron Corp Ltd

Chapter 4

Sheikh Sabah
Nasser Al-Sabah
Sheik Khaled Mohamed
Zayed Al-Nahyan
Yousef Mana
Saeed Al Otaiba
Nooni Mahmood
Eric Lim
Prof Hang Chang Chieh
Ho Sing
Ho Ching
Lee Hsien Loong
Khaldoon Khalifa Al Mubarak
Taib Mahmud
Liberace
Sulaiman Abdul Rahman Taib
Ian Sadler

National University of Singapore
Mubadala Investment Company
Cahaya Mata Sarawak (CMS)
RHB Group
Employees Provident Fund (EPF)

Kuwait Finance
House (KFH)
Utama Banking
Group (UBG)
Abu Dhabi Commercial Bank

Chapter 5

Azman Hashim
Hussain Najad
Ismail Ali
Tang Kee Chee aka
Casey Tang

Malayan Banking (Maybank)
Commerce International
Merchant Bankers (CIMB)
Hong Leong Banking (HLB)
Public Bank
RHB Bank Bhd
AmBank Bhd
Arab Malaysian
Development
Bank (AMDB)
Arab Investments for Asia
Kuwait Ltd (AIAK)
Malaysia Airlines (MAS)
Arab-Malaysian Merchant
Bank Holdings (AMMB)
Amcorp Berhad
Australia and New Zealand
Banking Group Ltd (ANZ)
Putrajaya Perdana
Loh & Loh Corp
AmInvestment Bank
Wynton Group
Khazanah Nasional
Majestic Masterpiece
RHB Bank

Chapter 6

Sultan Mizan Zainal Abidin
Tengku Rahimah Mahmud
Billal Shah
Rosmah Mansor
Nazir Razak
Roger Ng
Kee Kok Thiam
Teng Chean Choy
Chan Wan Seong
Joanna Yu
Cheah Tek Kuang
Jonathan Manifold
Cheah Teik Seng
Shahrol Azral Halmi
'Lancy Kwan'
Kok Tuck Cheong
Pushpa Rajadurai

Terengganu Investment
Authority (TIA)
BAE Systems Plc
BNP Paribas

Adkinson Securities, later renamed Country Group Securities
Shikumen Capital Management
Aktis Capital Singapore
United Overseas Bank (UOB)
Siam Commercial Bank
ACME Time Ltd
RBS Coutts Singapore

Chapter 7

Abdullah bin Abdulaziz
Prince Turki Abdullah
Tarek Obaid
Edward Lewis Morse

The Boston Consulting Group
JPMorgan
KPMG
Kadri Andri & Partner
Shearn Delamore & Co
Allen & Overy
Shook Lin & Bok
Ernst and Young
Merhav
Mossad
Minister of Finance Inc. aka MOF Inc.
1MDB Petrosaudi International
US State Department
Good Star Ltd

Chapter 8

Leonardo DiCaprio
Alicia Keys
Megan Fox
Miranda Kerr
Paris Hilton

Standard Chartered Bank
Price waterhouse Coopers (PwC)
Shearman & Sterling
Claridge's
The Connaught
The Berkeley

Chapter 9

Augustus Ralph Marshall
Sheikh Mansour bin Zayed Al Nayan
Tim Leissner

Accenture
Stanford University
Tanjong Tin Dredging Plc

MEASAT (Malaysia East Asia Satellite)
Manchester City
International Petroleum Investment Corp (IPIC)
Genting Group
Tenaga Nasional

Chapter 10

Datuk Azlin
Jamaluddin Jarjis
Saud Abdulaziz Al Saud
Ashok Ramamurthy
Azman Hashim
Prince Faisal bin Turkey Alsaud
Bob Mofatt
Nor Shamsiah Mohd Yunus

Blackstone Asia Real Estate Partners

Chapter 11

Rahah Mohamed Noah
Mukhriz Mahathir
Othman Saat
Musa Hitam

The Edge Review
Society of Publishers in Asia (Sopa)

Chapter 12

Xavier Andrew Justo
Patrick Mahoney
Laura
Christian Frampton
Clare Rewcastle Brown
Gordon Brown
Andrew Brown
Nurul Izzah Ibrahim
Tong Kooi Ong
Abdul Murad Khalid

BBC World Service
Sarawak Report
Royal Thai Police
Phileo Allied Group
United Overseas Bank Ltd
Phileo Allied Bank
Ayer Molek Rubber Company
Insas Bhd
The Edge

Chapter 13

Shaariibuugiin Altantuyaa
Abu Kassim Mohamed

Abdul Gani Patail
Tony Pua
Abdul Murad Khalid
Ho Kay Tat

Malaysian Anti-Corruption Commission (MACC)
The Edge Media Group
Justo Consulting Co Ltd
Democratic Action Party (DAP)
Bruno Manser Fund
Royal Thai Police

Chapter 14

Arul Kanda Kandasamy
Johari Abdul Ghani
Abdul Azeez Abdul Rahim
Rosman Abdullah
Khalid Abu Bakar
Ahmad Zahid Hamidi
Ali Hamza

The Wall Street Journal
Falcon Bank
SRC International Sdn Bhd
The Straits Times

Chapter 15

Apandi Ali
Ahmad Sazilee Abdul Khairi
Barack Obama
Frank White Jr
Kevin Morais
R. Kunaseegaran
Cheong Mei Kuen
Sei Ngan Chai

US Federal Bureau of Investigation (FBI)
White House
DuSable Capital Management
US Homeland Security
Malaysian Armed Forces
US Department of Justice
Park Lane Hotel
EMI

Chapter 16

Saifuddin Nasution Ismail
Wan Azizah Wan Ismail

Parti Pribumi Bersatu Malaysia (Bersatu)
Pakatan Harapan (PH or Alliance of Hope)
Parti Keadilan Rakyat (PKR or People's Justice Party)
Election Commission (EC)